DID YOU EVER THINK YOU COULD STOP FORECLOSURE?

An Essential Guide for Families Facing Financial Crisis

by

Christopher M. Lee, Esq.

Did You Ever Think You Could Stop Foreclosure? – An Essential Guide for Families Facing Financial Crisis

Christopher M. Lee, Esq.

Lee Law Firm, PLLC

8701 Bedford Euless Road
Suite 510
Hurst, Texas 76053
Tel: 817-265-0123

Visit Our Website at: www.leebankruptcy.com

A LEGAL NOTICE

Although I am going to provide a wealth of information in this book for families facing financial crisis, you must understand that this book does NOT constitute legal advice. Moreover, reading this book does NOT establish an attorney-client relationship between us. The only way to give you legal advice is for you to hire me. To retain my services, you must sign a written agreement, called a "Retainer Agreement". The retainer agreement sets forth the terms of my representation of you and the details of our attorney-client relationship, including the cost.

Only after you have hired me as your Attorney by signing a Retainer Agreement, will I be able to give you legal advice. Until that time, however, I can help you to educate yourself by providing you with some useful information about foreclosure, bankruptcy and dealing with your creditors.

ADVERTISEMENT

i
. . . .

TABLE OF CONTENTS

INTRODUCTION

FORECLOSURE TRUTHS!

Foreclosures Lead in U.S. Recession Statistics

Not since the Great Depression has our quest for the American Dream seemed so fruitless. With the unemployment rate having reached 10.2% in October 2009, many people are losing hope. They wonder will they ever find a job and if they find one, will they earn enough to take care of their families. Even for those who have found work, they are often working fewer hours for less money. And for those fortunate enough to have not been laid off, work furloughs and reduced wages may be in their future. According to the U.S. Bureau of Labor Statistics, wages, which account for about 70% of compensation, and benefits, which account for about 30% of compensation, are at their lowest reported levels since 1976.

This crisis is far reaching. Not only is it impacting blue collar workers in the construction, auto, and manufacturing industries, it's effecting white collar workers as well – lawyers, doctors, educators, and executives. The bottom line is that "job security" is a thing of the past. If an upper management executive earning $500,000 who's been with his company for over twenty years can get laid off, then any of us can. Entire communities are struggling with the consequences of unemployment and with more people competing for fewer jobs, the outlook for the future seems rather bleak.

The rising unemployment rate impacts the ability of homeowners to make their mortgage payments as is evidenced by the increase in foreclosures nationwide. According to RealtyTrac.com, in the third quarter of 2009, there were 937,840 foreclosure filings.[1] This is a 23% increase as compared to third quarter 2008 filings.

According to HousingPredictor.com, on average, every foreclosure costs the economy $225,000 and it is estimated that by the end of 2012, more than 10 million homeowners will have lost their homes to foreclosure. Moreover, the Mortgage Bankers Association has estimated that approximately 12% of American mortgages are delinquent or in the formal stages of foreclosure at any given time. Industry experts predict that by the end of 2010, more than 1/3 of the nation's loans will be "underwater".

These numbers are staggering and it's quite apparent that waiting around for Congress to formulate a strategy to help homeowners is not wise. The Obama Administration enacted legislation which gives lenders a $75 billion incentive to *voluntarily* modify mortgage loans in order to help homeowners avoid foreclosure.[2] Unfortunately, according to the Treasury Department, only about 12% of eligible homeowners have been offered modifications under the Making Home Affordable program and even fewer homeowners have accepted the assistance. Without a federal mandate *requiring* banks to modify loans to prevent foreclosures, HousingPredictor.com estimates that as many as 25% of homeowners with mortgages will eventually be foreclosed on. Whether legislation will be enacted which forces banks to modify loans for struggling homeowners is debatable. What we know is that most homeowners have no time to wait for a government solution. Therefore, they must be proactive and seek out solutions on their own.

The Baby-Boomer Population is Set to Retire Within the Next Ten Years

Within the next fifteen years, approximately 2/3 of the U.S. adult population will be reaching retirement age and will begin living on a fixed income. By 2020, it's estimated that more than 105 million adults will retire and begin drawing Social Security benefits. The big question is whether there will be enough funds in the Social Security till for these future retirees to draw from. If not, will they be forced to declare bankruptcy? Will these retired baby boomers be forced to take part-time jobs just to stay afloat? Indeed, for those baby boomers who are currently mired in debt and already having financial difficulties, the prospect of retirement is a very scary thing.

American Consumers Have Been Duped!

Americans have been dubbed by the credit card industry! Over the past thirty or so years, the credit card industry has convinced us that if we don't have a wallet full of credit cards, we are somehow unworthy. We're not successful. They've convinced us that the only type of gratification is instant gratification; saving for those big ticket items is no longer considered a responsible way of handling your finances.

Here's what we've been told: Why not just charge it? That way you can have your 52" high-definition plasma TV sitting in your family room today, right? Don't deny yourself the pleasure of that $2000 handbag or that $5000 refrigerator! You can pay it off over time. Sure, we'll charge you some interest, but only 7% or 8% because you have great credit. Go on, that shiny diamond pendant can be yours. . .right now. Just charge it!

Well, the credit card companies are not our friends. After lobbying for the bankruptcy laws to be changed to make it more difficult for consumers to file Chapter 7 cases, Congress enacted the Bankruptcy Abuse Prevention and Consumer Protection Act of 2005 (BAPCPA). Although this legislation did not have the desired effect (more Americans than ever are filing bankruptcy) the primary guiding principal behind it was to punish consumers who fell for the con laid on them by the credit card companies. Nowhere in the BAPCPA are creditors held responsible for giving credit cards to already overextended consumers. Nor are they held responsible for giving exorbitant credit lines to unemployed students.

To add insult to injury, in recent years, credit card companies have begun charging higher and higher fees – over the limit fees, late fees, non-use fees, and fees for paying off the balance each month. After Congress passed credit card legislation in 2009, the credit card companies went into overdrive raising interest rates, reducing credit lines, and otherwise sticking it to consumers in advance of the new laws becoming effective. The honest truth is that the banks are greedy and want to bleed American consumers for every penny they can possibly get! And remember, the banks created much of this economic mess in which we find ourselves presently mired.

Most of us have no idea how much credit card debt we have. We are clueless as to the interest rates we're paying on each of our credit cards. Suffice it to say that most of us have way more credit card debt than we can realistically afford. And if you're only making the minimum payment on your credit cards, it will be virtually impossible for you to pay them off in a reasonable period of time. During the Clinton Administration, America reached an economic high point. Jobs were plentiful, the stock market was doing quite well, and the average American felt financially secure and believed that their financial future looked bright. Over the past eight or nine years, things have changed drastically. Older Americans fear losing everything they've worked so hard for and younger Americans wonder if they'll have as good a life as their parents. The truth is that the middle class is shrinking and more and more Americans are looking poverty dead in the face. As things stand, the loss of a job, a major illness or injury, the death of a spouse, or a divorce is all it will take to push millions of Americans into the poor house.

The Hard Working Homeowner's Fate in a Dead Economy

The foreclosure rate has skyrocketed. No community has been left untouched. Losing a home to foreclosure is a devastating experience. Not only does it mean uprooting the family, it means the loss of the stability and comfort afforded by homeownership. It's a humiliating experience that often leads to feelings of anger and resentment and can result in depression for every member of the family.

Foreclosure also has a negative impact on communities. By some estimates, for each foreclosure in a neighborhood, surrounding homes lose 1%-2% of their value. There is also a stigma that attaches to a neighborhood if it has numerous foreclosures; prospective buyers think lots of foreclosures are a reflection on the residents in the neighborhood. Finally, when a home is being appraised, neighboring homes are used as comparables. Foreclosures are not arms length transactions and most appraisers will not use foreclosures as comparable if other arms length sales are available. However, if foreclosures are the only available comparables, an appraiser will use them and come back with an appraised value that is substantially lower than the seller anticipated.

Are You at Your Wits End?

Are you being constantly hounded by bill collectors? Are you robbing Peter to pay Paul? Are you behind on your mortgage payments and wondering how you'll ever get caught up? For many Americans who find themselves in financial crisis, ignoring the problem seems like the easiest thing to do. They know that it's not the wisest choice. But because they see no foreseeable improvement in their financial situation, short of winning the lottery, they go into a state of denial. Ignoring the problem won't change it. In fact, ignoring the problem will only make it worse. Late fees, over the limit fees, legal and collection fees loaded on to a debt can make it double or even triple in size virtually overnight!

A Beacon in a Storm!

Lee Law Firm is a beacon in the storm. If you are drowning in debt and feel helpless and alone, we can rescue you. We understand that you are overwhelmed and don't know how to go about solving your financial problems. We understand that the collection calls are driving you crazy. And we understand that it breaks your heart every time you have to tell your kids "no" because you don't have any extra money to buy pizza or go to the movies. Give us a call and we will help you find the right solution for *you*!

---

1   Foreclosure filings include default notices, auctions, and bank repossessions.

2   The legislation is known as the Making Home Affordable Act of 2009.

CHAPTER ONE

HOW DID YOU GET HERE AND WHAT ARE YOU GOING TO DO ABOUT IT?

1.1 A Quick Lesson in Home Loan Financing

Deregulation of the banking industry precipitated the current economic crisis. In the late 1990's, the Gramm-Leach-Bliley Act, which allowed mergers between commercial banks, insurance companies, and investment banks, became law.[3] Senator Phil Gramm can also be credited (or blamed) for passage of the Commodity Futures Modernization Act, which deregulated securities trading. As a lobbyist for UBS, Gramm successfully lobbied for passage of the Responsible Lending Act. Touted as anti-predatory lending legislation, consumer advocate took the position that the Responsible Lending Act essentially made loan sharking by banks and other financial institutions legal because it was designed to supersede stronger state laws prohibiting predatory lending.

Prior to deregulation, mortgage lenders sold loans on the secondary market to Fannie Mae and Freddie Mac. The existence of the secondary market was essential to the ongoing functioning of banks; without the secondary market, banks would have been required to wait for borrowers to pay off their loans before they could make additional loans. The secondary mortgage market system was predicated on two assumptions: 1) that loans would only be made to credit worthy borrowers and 2) the properties securing those loans had enough value to support them.

Deregulation had three closely related consequences. First, it allowed investors like Goldman Sachs, Bear Stearns, and Lehman Brothers, to name a few, to enter the secondary mortgage market, purchasing loans in much the same manner as Fannie Mae and Freddie Mac. Hence, the creation of a new investment vehicle – mortgage backed securities. Next, it fostered creative financing and predatory lending – stated income loans, low doc loans, no doc loans, interest only loans, adjustable rate mortgages, option adjustable rate mortgages – which gave rise to the booming subprime mortgage market. Finally, it paved the way for the creation of a collateral parcelization system where home loans were broken up into little components for sale on the secondary market.

The Calm Before the Storm

The growth of the subprime mortgage market was the calm before the storm. Banks and investors alike became intoxicated with the prospect of all the money to be made by buying and selling subprime mortgages on the secondary market. This frenzy to get a piece of the subprime mortgage pie turned to greed.

With little regard for whether borrowers could actually afford these loans and no regard for whether the property being purchased by the borrowers had sufficient value to fully collateralize the loans, many lenders loosened underwriting requirements to nearly non-existent levels. What difference did it make whether the borrower could actually afford the loan when there were literally dozens of investors angling to buy up pieces of as many loans as they possibly could?

What economists, banking executives, and politicians failed to acknowledge or chose to ignore was that there would come a time when many subprime borrowers would default. In 2006, as the teaser rates on adjustable rate mortgage began adjusting up and as principal payments on interest only loans kicked in, it became apparent that many subprime borrowers would simply be unable to make the higher mortgage payments and the number of defaults began increasing.

The other element to all of this is the fact that property values began decreasing almost simultaneously with the rise in borrower defaults. This catastrophic convergence of events was the perfect storm which brought us to our current economic state – huge unemployment rates, record foreclosure rates, tightened lending guidelines, decreasing property values, and a depressed real estate market.

Little did anyone realize that by the end of the first decade of the 21st century we would be in the midst of a recession. Average Americans, people just like you, find themselves teetering on the edge of a financial precipice. Faced with adjustable rate mortgage re-sets and an inability to refinance into fixed rate loans, ever-increasing credit card interest rates and fees, multiple auto loans, and a host of other debts which are drowning them, these consumers are desperately searching for a financial life preserver. But what happens when something unexpected – something catastrophic – happens?

1.1.1 What Happens When a Family Experiences a Job Loss?

In the past, when a worker was laid off or injured on the job, the employer typically provided resources until government benefits, such as unemployment or disability payments, kicked in. Family and friends could be counted on to rally around the family until the bread winner found a new job or recovered from his injury. A job loss or work-related injury was not the end of the world because the extended family and the community pooled their resources when one of their own needed assistance.

What's different about the current crisis is that many people in the same family and in the same community have lost their jobs. Because everyone is struggling, there are fewer resources available for pooling. Everyone is looking for a helping hand. We see this in the growing number of people turning to food banks and other social service programs for assistance. And even these agencies are struggling to meet the demand. It appears that even our resources are out of resources!

Long term unemployment and underemployment can have a devastating impact on a family. For many families who have lost income as a result of unemployment and underemployment, bankruptcy is the only option.

1.1.2 What Happens When Divorce Impacts a Family?

Regardless of the circumstances, divorce (and separation) usually has a tremendous impact on a family, from both a psychological and a financial standpoint. Unfortunately, financial difficulties can precipitate the decision to divorce. Couples who are having financial problems are stressed out and worried and as a result tend to argue more, not only about money, but about everything else as well. When a couple is struggling to pay their bills, any other problems they might be experiencing seem to become magnified in importance and intensity.

Divorce results in a reduction of household income for both spouses. After divorce, each spouse must find a means of maintaining their respective households. Marital assets and debts will be divided, not necessarily equally, between the divorcing spouses. Non-custodial parents must also pay child support and in some instances, one spouse may be ordered to pay alimony (spousal support) to the other spouse. Because of the financial burdens resulting from divorce, one or both spouses may find themselves contemplating bankruptcy.

1.1.3 What Happens When Tragedy Hits a Family?

When a family member takes ill, experiences a catastrophic injury, or passes, the impact on the entire family is quite devastating. The emotional toll that a long term illness or major injury takes on the patient and his loved ones can be overwhelming. Accumulating medical bills only add to the stress and heartache the family is experiencing. That stress and heartache are compounded when the loved one passes.

The financial impact of a long term illness, catastrophic injury, or death of a family member can be tremendous. This is especially true when the illness, injury, or death results in the loss of household income. Not only has the household income decreased, debt is accumulating as the medical bills (and funeral bills) begin pouring in. For many families who have experienced such a tragedy, getting out of debt and returning to a place of financial and emotional stability often seems nearly impossible.

1.1.4 What Happens When Your Interest Rate Re-sets?

For many homeowners, it wasn't a job loss, divorce, or tragedy that pushed them to the edge of financial ruin. It was a re-set of the interest rate on their mortgage that caused the problem. Between 2000 and 2006, multitudes of borrowers realized the dream of homeownership because subprime lending made it possible for many people, who previously could not qualify for a mortgage loan, to qualify. The majority of the subprime loans made during this time period, were adjustable rate loans. These loans offered low interest rates that were fixed for three to five years. At the end of that three to five year period, the lender was free to raise the interest rate as often as every six months. More over, a large percentage of these loans were interest only loans, which required borrowers to pay only the interest which accrued during the period when the interest rate was fixed. So, at the end of that three to five year period, not only did the interest rate go up, borrowers were also required to begin paying *principal **and** interest.*

For many homeowners, a mortgage re-set results in a doubling or even a tripling of their monthly mortgage payment. It's no wonder the mortgage default and foreclosure rates have skyrocketed.

At the beginning of the mortgage meltdown, many homeowners thought they'd be able to refinance into fixed rate mortgages and avoid the interest rate re-set. Little did they know, lenders had already begun tightening up lending requirements. Thus, making it very difficult for these borrowers, who had credit problems or no proof of income when they originally obtained the mortgage, to refinance.

As the foreclosure rate began rising, property values began decreasing. As a result, many homeowners are "underwater" – they owe more on their homes that what they are worth. This makes selling a home very difficult because potential buyers are unwilling to pay more than the home is worth, lenders certainly won't lend more than the home is worth, and most sellers don't have cash available to pay off the difference at closing.

1.1.4.1 Cultural Changes Inside the Mortgage Industry, Deregulation, and Wall Street Greed

Before deregulation, banks focused on two principles when making mortgage loans: 1) whether a borrower was credit worthy and 2) whether the collateral (the property being purchased) had enough value to fully secure the loan. If the answer to either question was "no", the borrower's loan application was denied. Banks were very risk averse and in an effort to manage or reduce risk, they used strict underwriting guidelines when making mortgage loans.

Deregulation changed lending practices and fostered a culture of greed. Lenders became less concerned with whether a borrower could afford to repay the loan and whether the value of the property supported the loan because they knew investors on the secondary market were anxiously waiting to buy up as many mortgages as they could. The more new loans a lender could sell on the secondary market, the more money it would have available to lend.

Deregulation allowed Wall Street brokerage firms to jump into the secondary mortgage market and buy up mortgages in much the same way as Freddie Mac and Fannie Mae were doing prior to deregulation. The brokerages would then sell pieces of these loans, known as mortgage backed securities, to their investors. And everyone was happy because tons of money was being made. But the question was: "How can we make even more money?" Well, creative lenders had the answer to that question. They developed various loan products which made it possible for virtually anyone to be approved for a mortgage. These products included stated income, verified asset loans (SIVA), no income, verified assets loans (NIVA), and no income, no asset loans (NINA).

SIVA loans allowed borrowers to simply show that they had money in the bank and to state their income. The lender did not verify the borrower's income. NIVA loans required that borrowers only prove they had money in the bank. Lenders were not in the least concerned with the source of those funds. NINA loans required borrowers to prove nothing; lenders simply looked at the borrower's credit score and if it was high enough, their loan application would be approved.

Lenders no longer cared about managing the risk because of the ease with which mortgages could be sold on the secondary market. The investors who were buying up these loans believed they were making sound investments because Standard & Poor's and other credit rating agencies gave mortgage back securities such high ratings.[4]

---

3   The Gramm-Leach-Bliley Act was the brain-child of then Senator Phil Gramm who after leaving the Senate went on to work for UBS as a lobbyist. Gramm later became Senator John McCain's chief economic advisor and co-chair of McCain's 2008 presidential campaign.

4   The higher the credit rating, the less risky an investment is considered to be. Mortgage backed securities were typically given AAA ratings, which meant that they were about the safest investment a person could make

CHAPTER TWO

Foreclosure Rescue and
Loan Modification Scams

With the number of foreclosures on the rise and more and more homeowners facing financial uncertainty, the scam artists have come out of the woodwork offering to stop foreclosures or to modify loans. These scammers prey on desperate homeowners who are looking for a way to save their homes from foreclosure. They use half truths, outright lies, threats, and scare tactics to take advantage of distressed homeowners.

2.1 Common Scams

Foreclosure rescue and loan modification scam artists engage in various schemes to bilk homeowners out of what money they have and, in many cases, these scammers actually manage to con the homeowner into signing over the deed to their home. The goal is to make a quick profit and then move on to the next victim.

The most common foreclosure rescue scams include:

- Rent-to-buy where the homeowner is told that an investor will purchase the property and rent it back to the homeowner until he can afford to buy it back;

- Equity skimming where the scam artist promises to find a

buyer for the home on the condition that the owner quit claims the property to him. After the homeowner signs the quitclaim deed, the scam artist rents the property and pockets the rent until the homeowner's lender forecloses;

- Phantom help where the scammer promises counseling or other assistance in exchange for payment of an up-front fee by the homeowner;

- Bait and switch where the scammer convinces the home owner to sign loan documents which supposedly contain more favorable loan terms when in actuality they transfer title to the property in exchange for a "rescue loan";

- Fraudulent bankruptcy filing where, in exchange for an up-front fee, the scammer promises to handle all negotiations with the lender as long as the homeowner stops communicating with the lender. No negotiations take place, the scammer files bankruptcy in the homeowner's name, which stops calls from the mortgage company. Because the home owner is unaware of the bankruptcy filing, the case eventually gets dismissed and the lender forecloses;

- Partial interest bankruptcy where the scam artist has the homeowner transfer a partial interest in the property to several different people who then each file for bankruptcy back-to-back; the homeowner is directed to remit his mortgage payments to the scammer who doesn't forward the payments to the lender. The automatic stay goes into effect with each filing, but only serves to temporarily delay the foreclosure until the lender receives permission from the court to foreclose.

2.2 Recent Scams in the News

Practically everyday, law enforcement agencies shut down and/or prosecute foreclosure rescue and loan modification scam operations. In April, 2009, the FTC in conjunction with the attorney generals in several states targeted dozens of companies which used deceptive practices to market their services, including giving the false impression that they are affiliated with HUD and other federal agencies. Legal action has been taken against various scammers across the country. The following is a short list of scam operations which have been targeted:

- September, 2009 – Foreclosure rescue scammer Rosario Castro Divins of San Antonio Texas was sentenced to 350 months in prison by U.S. District Court judge;

- October, 2009 - Wisconsin Attorney General sued California based 21st Century Legal Services, Inc. alleging violations of state law pertaining to soliciting and sell loan modification services to Wisconsin homeowners;

- October, 2009 – Idaho Department of Finance issued a cease and desist order against International Co-op, LLC for engaging in unlicensed loan modification activities and for charging excessive up-front fees;

- October, 2009 – Arizona Attorney General wins $1.37

million in penalties and restitution against Taken Care of Investments, LLC and Hope for Homeowners Now, LLC arising from foreclosure rescue and loan modification scams;

- November, 2009 – California State Bar announced that its loan modification task force obtained the resignations of three attorneys as a result of their misconduct in relation to loan modification services they offered. Another attorney's license was suspended as a result of similar misconduct and license suspensions are pending for two other attorneys who are believed to have engaged in loan modification scams;

- November, 2009 – Florida Attorney General sued National Payment Modification Company and The Bostonian Group, LLC alleging they charged upfront fees for foreclosure rescue services;

- November, 2009 – Texas Attorney General obtained a temporary injunction against Markus and Tyrone Bailey to halt operations of Behind on Mortgage and Behind on Mortgage USA, two unlicensed businesses offering foreclosure rescue services.

2.3 How to Avoid Foreclosure Rescue and Loan Modification Scams

Foreclosure rescue and loan modification scammers, like other con artists, use homeowners' desperation and fears against them. However, there are a number of red flags that all distressed homeowners should be aware of when making contact with anyone offering foreclosure rescue or loan modification assistance.

- Requiring payment of up-front fees (this is illegal in some states);
- Guaranteeing that the foreclosure can be stopped;
- Advising the homeowner to stop communicating with their lender, attorney, and credit counselor;
- Only accepting payment in the form of a cashier's check or wire transfer;
- Requiring the homeowner to make his mortgage payment directly to the foreclosure rescue or loan modification company;
- Requiring the homeowner to transfer title to his property to the company or an investor;
- Offering to or insisting on completing the paperwork for the homeowner;
- Insisting that the homeowner give power of attorney to an employee of the company;
- Pressuring the homeowner to sign documents he hasn't read or does not understand;
- Refusing to allow the homeowner to have the documents reviewed by an attorney before he signs them.

Homeowners should also be wary of any solicitations which say things like: *"Stop Foreclosure Immediately"*, *"Guaranteed Loan Modification Assistance"*, *"Guaranteed Results – We Stop*

Foreclosures Everyday". Scammers often scour the county real estate records for Notices of Default and use that information to target distressed homeowners with these types of direct mail pieces.

2.4 Protect Yourself from Scammers

The best way to protect yourself from foreclosure rescue and loan modification scams is to know who you are dealing with. You should contact the Better Business Bureau or your state consumer protection group to determine whether the company has had any complaints filed against it. Rather than responding to solicitations you receive in the mail, it's best to contact a HUD approved housing counselor to get assistance.

Never sign documents you haven't read or don't understand. You have a right to have any documents you may sign reviewed by an attorney before you sign them. Make sure that all information about the services being offered are in writing and signed by the person providing the services. Oral promises and agreements pertaining to your home are not legally binding. Insist on getting copies of all contracts and be sure to keep copies of all documents you sign and submit to the service provider.

Never convey ownership of your home to the service provider or a third party. Legitimate companies will never ask you to do this and it is not necessary to save your home from foreclosure or effectuate a loan modification. Moreover, make your mortgage payments only to the lender or loan servicer.

If you are looking for assistance in saving your home from foreclosure, its best to hire an attorney. Attorneys must follow a code of conduct and they are monitored by the state bar. If an attorney engages in illegal, questionable, or unethical conduct in relation to their clients, the client may seek redress with the state bar. The state bar will investigate the client's allegations and if it finds that the attorney has acted improperly, it will sanction the attorney accordingly.

2.5 Report Suspicious Activity

If you believe you have been or are currently being victimized by a scammer, you must take action immediately because these scammers often disappear overnight. You can report suspicious activity to the Federal Trade Commission by calling 1-877-FTC-HELP (1-877-382-4357). You can also report scammers to the Office of the Attorney General in your state or to your state or local consumer protection agency.

2.6 Review

The thought of foreclosure is terrifying. The prospect of losing the place you and your family call home is scary no matter how you look at it. So, the possibility of being scammed by a low-down dirty con artist is simply heinous. Therefore, no matter how helpless and desperate you feel, you simply cannot place your trust in the first person who comes along offering to help you.

Foreclosure rescue and loan modification scams are rampant. Any homeowner facing foreclosure must be vigilant and use common sense when investigating solutions offered by these companies. Trust your gut if something just doesn't seem right. Don't let anyone pressure you into signing documents or making hasty decisions. And be especially cautious of paying up-front fees.

. . . .

CHAPTER THREE

The Role of Predatory Lending & Mortgage Fraud in the Declining Real Estate Market

"Predatory Lending" is defined as "the industry-based professional practice of using a borrower's ignorance of lending practices
against them for profit."[5] In recent years, the number of predatory
residential mortgage loans has grown dramatically. Minority and
poor borrowers are particularly susceptible to predatory lending
because they are less knowledgeable about lending practices. Additionally, according to the FBI, real estate fraud continues to surge
forward, with reports of mortgage fraud having tripled in the last
two years. The dollar value attached to these crimes has also
quadrupled to over one billion dollars! The number of fraud cases
investigated by the FBI is "not keeping pace with the rise in
reports." The Bureau's conviction rate has fallen from a national
total of 256 in 2003 to 170 in 2008.

Mortgage fraud in its simplest forms involves a borrower who
lies on his loan application or provides phony bank statements or
pay stubs. More complex cases of mortgage fraud involve a ring
of conspirators including the appraiser, loan officer, mortgage bro-

ker, closing attorney, and *"straw buyers"*. These mortgage fraud rings use inflated appraisals and forged sales contracts to dupe unsuspecting homeowners out of their homes, often leaving them with huge capital gains tax bills for profits they did not actually receive when the property was sold.

In the majority of mortgage fraud cases involving straw buyers, the property is never occupied and few, if any, mortgage payments are made. Eventually the lender forecloses. If enough mortgage fraud foreclosures take place in the same neighborhood, it has a devastating impact on property values.[6] The aftermath of mortgage fraud is one reason many homeowners are upside down in their mortgages.

Subprime loans make up a large majority of predatory loans.[7] The Center for Responsible Lending recently examined a batch of sub-prime loans which had been sold to investors in a securitization package, and reported that "the majority of loans were subprime loans with terms that have been key drivers in the current epidemic of foreclosures."[8]

---

5   www.wikipedia.org, Predatory Lending definition

6   The Water's Edge Subdivision in Stone Mountain, DeKalb County, GA was especially hard hit by mortgage fraud between 2002 and 2006.

7   According to Standard & Poor's, subprime mortgages made accounted for 16.8% of all mortgage loans made in 2006.

8   The Center for Responsible Lending report

CHAPTER FOUR

When Refinancing Is No Longer An Option

Because of current economic conditions, refinancing is no longer an option for many homeowners. For these homeowners, finding alternate options is critical if they're to have any hope of stopping the foreclosure.

Possible options include:

- Short Sale
- Deed in Lieu of Foreclosure
- Loan Modification

Short Sale – For homeowners who are unable to refinance, whose request for loan modification has been denied, and for whom the other foreclosure avoidance options are not feasible, a short sale may be the best choice. A short sale is a negotiated remedy between a borrower and his lender whereby the lender agrees to accept as a full payoff of the loan less than what is actually owed on it. If either party is unwilling to agree to the other parties proposed terms, the short sale will not happen and the lender will proceed with the fore-closure. Borrowers are advised to demand that the lender provide them with a written statement that upon receipt of the agreed upon payoff amount by the lender, the borrower will be relieved of any further liability under the loan agreement (the Promissory Note). In other words, the lender will not pursue a deficiency judgment against the borrower or otherwise seek to collect the short fall from the borrower.

Deed in Lieu of Foreclosure – A deed in lieu of foreclosure is another negotiated remedy. If the lender agrees to accept a deed in lieu of foreclosure, the borrower will sign a document which transfers title to the property to the lender. As with a short sale, the borrower should demand written confirmation that upon execution and delivery of the deed in lieu of foreclosure to the lender, he will be relieved of any further obligation under the Note.

Loan Modification – Loan modification is yet another negotiated remedy. The typical loan modification involves a change to one or more terms of the loan to make it more affordable to the borrower. The borrower will be required to sign documents which memorialize the changes to the loan. If the borrower and lender cannot agree on new terms, the lender is free to move forward with foreclosure proceedings if the borrower does not cure the default.

If you begin exploring these options before you default on your mortgage, chances are that one of them may actually work. The problem, though, is that most homeowners go into a state of denial about their financial problems. They think that they'll be able to get caught up on their mortgage and their other bills in just a few weeks. Maybe they're waiting for a windfall of some sort. Regardless of how they think they'll be able to resolve their money woes, by the time most homeowners come to their senses and face the fact that they are really in trouble, it's much too late to explore selling the property. Moreover, despite the claims of the media and big banks like Bank of America and Chase, lenders are very slow to actually approve loan modification. So, where does that leave the average homeowner? It leaves them with a Notice of Default, a looming foreclosure, and no solution! The good news is that you don't have to wait for your lender to agree to help you. You can take a giant step toward solving your financial problems and saving your home from foreclosure. You have more control than you know!

4.1 Regaining Control of Your Life

The first step in regaining control of your life is to admit that you have a problem. Take a moment to answer these questions:

- Are you 30 days or more behind on your mortgage payments? Yes or No
- Are you 30 days or more behind on your car payments? Yes or No
- Are you using your credit cards to buy necessities like food and gasoline? Yes or No
- Are all of your credit cards close to or over their limits? Yes or No
- Do you only make the minimum payment on your credit cards each month? Yes or No
- Do you pay your credit card payments late each month? Yes or No

- Are you 30 days or more behind on any of your credit cards? Yes or No
- Have you gotten a payday loan within the past three months? Yes or No
- Have you received collection letters or phone calls within the past month? Yes or No
- Have been sued by any of your creditors within the past 30 days? Yes or No

If you answered "yes" to at least three of these questions, warning bells should be going off because a financial crisis is right around the corner. If you answered yes to five or more of these questions, you are obviously drowning in debt and need someone to rescue you - *NOW!*.

Whether you are headed toward a financial disaster or are already in the midst of it, the next step in regaining control of your life is to put together an action plan. Your action plan must include an honest breakdown of your income and spending habits as well as what steps you will take to pay your debts.

4.1.1 Control Does Not Mean You Must Go It Alone

Many homeowners wait to seek out help because they are ashamed and embarrassed to be in such a precarious financial situation. In my many years of practice, I've come to realize that bad things happen to good people. So, there's not need to be ashamed.

Most people don't actively choose the circumstances, such as a job loss or illness, which have brought them to the brink of foreclosure. Even for those who are facing foreclosure because they haven't been as prudent with their financial decisions as they could have been, there's nothing to be ashamed of. After all, we're all human and we all make mistakes.

So, please don't wait a moment longer. Decide in this moment to seek out professional help and begin formulating a plan to get back on the right track.

4.1.2 Creating Solution-Oriented Partnerships

Finding the right partners to help you formulate a plan is key to resolving your financial issues. A debt counselor can help you review your finances and create a budget. For some, a realistic budget is all they need to begin digging themselves out of the financial hole they're in. For others, however, more drastic measures, like bankruptcy, may be necessary.

If you believe bankruptcy is the right choice for you, you need an experienced and dedicated bankruptcy attorney on your side. Your attorney should not take a cookie-cutter approach to your case, but should treat you and your circumstances as unique, crafting a bankruptcy strategy that will maximize your chances of regaining your financial footing as quickly and painlessly as possible.

4.1.3 De-stressing Your Life

As you begin the process of regaining control of your life, you will notice that your stress level will begin going down. As good as it will feel to be able to get a good night's sleep or to have dinner each evening uninterrupted by harassing phone call from creditors and bill collectors, you've got to make a commitment to changing your lifestyle. This commitment begins with taking stock of how you spend your money. Ask yourself whether you have been living above your means. Where can you cut back on your spending? If you had been living a more modest lifestyle would that job loss, illness, divorce, or death in the family have impacted you as drastically as it did?

Because most Americans have bought into the instant gratification mindset, they are living above their means and most are only a paycheck or two away from homelessness. So, shifting your mindset is essential. It won't be easy to give up those extravagances and luxuries to which you become so accustomed. But in the long run, having financial security and knowing that you're prepared for the proverbial "rainy day" will give you a sense of peace and contentment.

9   The following states only allow judicial foreclosure: Connecticut, Delaware, Florida, Illinois, Indiana, Iowa, Kansas, Kentucky, Louisiana, Maine, North Dakota, New Jersey, New Mexico (non-judicial foreclosure allowed on commercial properties), Ohio, Pennsylvania, and South Carolina. Idaho and the District of Columbia are the only two states where non-judicial fore closure is the only option.

10   The following states allow a lender to use either judicial or non-judicial foreclosure: Alabama, Alaska, Arizona, Arkansas, California, Colorado, Georgia, Hawaii, Maryland, Massachusetts, Michigan, Minnesota, Mississippi, Missouri, Montana, North Carolina, Nebraska, New Hampshire, New York, Nevada, Oklahoma, Oregon, South Dakota, Tennessee, Texas, Utah, Virginia, Vermont, Washington, West Virginia, Wisconsin, and Wyoming.

11   If you are not in the Tarrant County area, we would be happy to refer you to an attorney in your area who is as committed to helping families as Lee Law Firm.

CHAPTER FIVE

Saving Your Home From Foreclosure: You Can Fight Back!

Initially, when the average person has a financial problem, they think they can fix it themselves. It's a temporary problem and with a little creative accounting, they're sure they will be able to get out of that financial hole. As time passes, if the problem hasn't been resolved, some people will go into a state of denial. Others will turn to their family and friends for assistance. Regardless of whether the crisis is a result of an illness, divorce, or the loss of a job, eventually the average person will seek help from those who are closest to him. In the past, we had a strong support system and we'd pool our resources to help those in our extended family and in our community when they were in need. But what happens when the members of your support system and those in your community are also in crisis? Who do you turn to when you've missed several mortgage payments and your lender is threatening to foreclose?

5.1 Important Players In the Foreclosure Process

Knowing who the players are as you work to save your home

from foreclosure is critical. Some of these players will truly be on your side, while others may only be out to hurt you. The former will advocate for you and work diligently to help you obtain the best possible outcome under the circumstances. The latter prey on homeowners just like you - homeowners who are desparate to stop the foreclosure and save their homes.

5.1.1 Mortgage Companies, Investors, and Mortgage Servicers

Do you know the difference between a mortgage company, an investor, and a mortgage servicer? Most people don't. It's critical to understand who these entities are and the role they play in your efforts to save your home from foreclosure.

The Mortgage Company

The mortgage company (think bank) is the entity that originally lent you the money to purchase your home. In some instances, your  lender will also service your loan. Loan servicing entails collecting mortgage payments, managing escrow accounts, paying taxes and insurance from those escrow accounts, and otherwise overseeing all aspects of the loan until it is paid in full.

Investors

Investors purchase loans from mortgage companies and banks. To effectuate the purchase and sale of a loan, the mortgage company should execute and record an Assignment of Mortgage. Unfortunately, this step is often skipped when a mortgage is sold. Nevertheless, once an investor has paid for a loan, that investor "owns" the loan and has a legal right to collect the payments on that loan.

Mortgage Servicers

Mortgage servicers are hired by mortgage companies and investors to manage the collection of mortgage payments as well as other functions attendant to owning a mortgage loan. Mortgage servicers have no legal ownership interest in the loans they service and act only with the consent of the lenders and investors for whom they work. If you're dealing with a mortgage servicer be aware that the servicer has no decision making authority. The servicer must get approval for any loan modification, short sale, forbearance, etc. from the investor or mortgage company for whom it works.

Collections Department

The collections department of your mortgage company or mortgage servicer will take over your account when you have missed a mortgage payment. The role of the collection department is to get you to bring your mortgage payments current.

Foreclosure Department

The foreclosure department takes over once your loan has been accelerated and is officially in default. The foreclosure department works with the mortgage company's foreclosure attorney and handles your account until you cure the default, file bankruptcy, or sell the property.

Bankruptcy Department

If you file bankruptcy, the bankruptcy department will take over your account. The bankruptcy department coordinates with the mortgage company's bankruptcy attorney until your bankruptcy case is dismissed or you receive a discharge.

Loss Mitigation Department

The loss mitigation department is the only department than can approve a loan modification, short sale, forbearance agreement or other workout. Keep in mind that loss mitigation departments at most mortgage companies and mortgage servicers are swamped. Therefore, you may not get the timely response that you deserve. You must stay on top of your case and be persistent.

5.1.2 Community Advocates

There are numerous non-profit organizations across the country which specialize in assisting people who are in financial crisis. Some of these groups are geared specifically toward assisting homeowners who are facing foreclosure. Other groups provide social services such as food, job training, and medical services. For a list of community advocacy groups in the Tarrant County area, visit www.leebankruptcy.com.

5.1.3 Foreclosure Assistance Companies

In the past 18 months or so, hundreds, if not thousands, of foreclosure assistance companies have appeared offering to help home-owners save their homes from foreclosure. Some of these companies are legitimate. As discussed in Chapter Two, many of them are not. Therefore, before paying anyone offering to stop your home from being foreclosed on, check them out thoroughly!

5.1.4 Attorneys

An experienced attorney is your best tool in negotiating a work-out with your lender, fighting a foreclosure on legal grounds, or stopping a foreclosure by filing bankruptcy. Remember, the unauthorized practice of law is prohibited in all fifty states. This means that only a licensed attorney may provide legal services and give legal advice. Therefore, you should only hire a licensed attorney as you work to resolve your financial issues and save your home from foreclosure.

5.2 You've Received a Notice of Default – What's Next?

When a borrower defaults on a mortgage loan and fails to cure the default, the lender will mail the borrower a Notice of Default or Notice of Acceleration. This notice is the final step before the foreclosure process begins. It tells the borrower how much is owed on the mortgage and demands payment in full within a specified period of time. This is the last chance for the borrower to cure the default and avoid foreclosure.

Once the lender or servicer puts the Notice of Default in the mail, it's only concern is with getting its money or recovering its property. That's right – *IT'S PROPERTY*! Although most of us think of our homes as belonging to us, until we payoff the mortgage, the bank really owns it. It is the collateral for the mortgage loan and if a borrower defaults, the lender has a legal right to recover that collateral via the foreclosure process.

Once you receive a notice of default, it's imperative that you get the legal advice you need so that you make the decisions that will best protect your legal interests. Foreclosure is a very scary thought, but you don't have to face it alone.

5.3 Foreclosure – A Simple Definition

Foreclosure is the legal process whereby a mortgage lender or bank repossesses a home as a result of a borrower's default under the terms of the loan. The most common type of default that results in foreclosure is a failure to make mortgage payments. Other events of default which may result in foreclosure include failure to occupy the property (on loans where owner occupancy is a requirement), failure to pay homeowners association dues or property taxes, failure to maintain the property, and mortgage fraud. Of these other events of default, mortgage fraud is the only one which typically results in foreclosure.

State law governs how foreclosures are conducted in each state. There are two common types of foreclosure: judicial and non-judicial. Judicial foreclosure, as its name implies, requires a lender to file a lawsuit and receive an order from the court authorizing the foreclosure sale. A judicial foreclosure can take a year or more before it is completed. Non-judicial foreclosures, on the other hand, take as little as 21 days, depending upon the jurisdiction, and give a lender the right to foreclosure as long as it has complied with the state's legal requirements governing non-judicial foreclosures. Texas is a non-judicial foreclosure state.

There are also two lesser known methods of foreclosure: strict foreclosure and entry and possession foreclosure. These methods of foreclosure are available in only a few states and are rarely used in those states where they are available.

Strict foreclosure is available to lenders in Connecticut, New Hampshire, and Vermont. To move forward with a strict foreclosure, a lender must file a lawsuit alleging that the borrower has defaulted. If successful in proving a default by the borrower, the court will enter an order requiring the borrower to pay the mortgage within a specified period of time. If the borrower fails to do so, title to the property is transferred to the lender. Once a lender gets title to the property via strict foreclosure, it is under no legal obligation to sell it.

Entry and possession foreclosure is authorized under the laws of the states of New Hampshire, Maine, Massachusetts, and Vermont. This type of foreclosure allows a lender to peacefully enter and take possession of a property after a default by the borrower. The lender must maintain continuous possession of the property for a period of time specified by state law at the end of which it will have legal title to the property. During the period of possession, the lender must account for all rents and profits which may be offset by the expenses of maintaining the property. Entry and possession foreclosure is often used as a back-up in the event there was a technical error in the non-judicial sale process.

5.4 The Impact of a Foreclosure Can Be Devastating

The impact of a foreclosure can be devastating for a family. Foreclosure represents a loss of stability and security. Not only is it embarrassing and humiliating, foreclosure causes lots of upheaval and uncertainty for a family. Where will we live? How will foreclosure impact our credit and our ability to find a new home? Where will the kids go to school? What will happen to all of our belongings? What will our neighbors, friends, and family be saying about us?

5.4.1 The Financial Burden of Losing Your Home

Foreclosure creates both a short-term and a long-term financial burdens for a family. Immediately before or after a foreclosure, the family must find a place to live. This usually means renting which often entails paying a security deposit and the first month's rent. Depending on the laws of the state in which the family lives, it may also entail advance payment of the last month's rent as well. The family may also have to pay deposits in order to have the utilities in the rental property turned on. There are also the expenses associated with the move – renting a moving truck or hiring professional movers and renting a storage space if the rental property is too small to hold an entire household's worth of furniture.

Late payments, missed payments, and foreclosure can result in a cumulative loss of over 400 points on a person's score. Moreover, foreclosure stays on a person's credit report for as long as ten years. During the first few years after a foreclosure, a person will have some difficulty getting credit and will pay significantly higher interest rates on any extensions of credit which may be granted to him. This again can impact the family's ability to secure new housing or to purchase large ticket items such as a car. Additionally, because many employers check the credit of prospective employees, a foreclosure may impact a person's ability to secure employment.

5.4.2 Emotional Fallout

As humble as a home may be, for most people it represents a place of comfort and security. Moreover, most people derive a sense of pride from owning a home. The feelings of humiliation and the stress associated with foreclosure often lead to depression. For children in families facing foreclosure, confusion and depression are also very common. Studies show that children of foreclosure often believe that they are somehow to blame for the loss of the home. Because they don't want to be a burden to their parents, these children tend to internalize their feelings which can manifest in physical symptoms such as headaches and stomachaches.

Children are not the only ones who experience physical symptoms as a result of foreclosure. The stress and depression adults experience often manifest in headaches, stomachaches, increased blood pressure, loss of appetite, sleeplessness, and a myriad of other symptoms which impact a person's overall health. Many adults turn to alcohol and drugs in an effort to manage the stress they are feeling while dealing with a foreclosure.

5.5   Understanding   the   Foreclosure Process

As previously discussed, the two most common forms of foreclosure are judicial foreclosure and non-judicial foreclosure. State law determines which form of foreclosure lenders may use. In a minority of states, only one type of foreclosure is authorized.[9] Thirty-one states allow lenders to utilize either judicial or non-judicial foreclosure.[10]

5.5.1 How Judicial Foreclosures Work

A lender initiates a judicial forclosure by filing a complaint with the court in the county where the property is located. The complaint must allege, among other things, that the borrower has defaulted on a loan. After the homeowner is served with a copy of the complaint, he has an opportunity to file an answer which should set forth all defenses as well as any counterclaims he may have against the lender. At the hearing, the judge will hear evidence and testimony from the lender and the borrower. If the judge finds in favor of the lender, a judgment for the full amount due on the loan, including principal, interest, late fees, escrow overages, and attorney's fees will be entered. After entry of the judgment, a writ will be issued authorizing a sheriff's auction. Anyone may bid at the sheriff's sale and the property will be sold to the highest bidder, subject to the court's confirmation of the sale. The sales price must be paid in cash or by certifed check. Once the sale has been confirmed, the sheriff will execute and record a Sheriff's Deed conveying title to the property to the winning bidder.

If the amount received at the sheriff's sale is insufficient to pay-off the judgment in full, the lender may have a right to pursue a deficiency judgment against the borrower. To obtain a deficiency judgment, the lender must file a lawsuit against the borrower. The borrower may file an answer and at the hearing, the judge will make a decision after hearing testimony from both parties. If the lender proves its case, a judgment in the amount of the deficiency will be entered against the borrower. At that point, the lender may pursue any collection efforts authorized by state law, including garnishment.

The procedures for conducting a judicial foreclosure and obtaining a deficiency judgment vary from state to state. If you live outside of Texas, you should contact a real estate, foreclosure, or bankruptcy attorney in your area to get more information about how foreclosures in your state work.

5.5.2 How Non-Judicial Foreclosures Work

Non-judicial foreclosure laws authorize a lender to proceed with recovering property from a defaulting borrower without the necessity of going to court. Although the specific procedures for conducting a non-judicial foreclosure vary from state to state, lenders must generally give the borrower (and other interested parties, such as junior lien holders) written notice of the sale a few weeks before the sale is to take place. A foreclosing lender may also be required to record a Notice of Default in the real estate records of the county in which the property is located. Additionally, some states require that a notice of foreclosure be published in the legal organ of the county in which the property is located.

Once all notice requirements have been met, the lender will conduct an auction, usually on the courthouse steps, and the property will be sold to the highest bidder. The purchase price must be paid in cash or by certified check. Once the purchase price has been paid in full, a Power of Sale Deed or Foreclosure Deed conveying title to the property to the highest bidder will be executed and recorded in the county deed records.

5.6 How Foreclosures Work in Texas

Texas is one of thirty-one states in which lenders may utilize either the judicial foreclosure or the non-judicial foreclosure process. Most lenders choose the non-judical foreclosure process because it is less expensive and concludes much more quickly that the judicial foreclosure process.

The non-judicial foreclosure process in Texas is very short. Once a borrower defaults, the foreclosure sale can take place in as little as 60 days. In Texas, a lender initiates a non-judicial foreclosure by serving the debtor with a Notice of Default. The Notice of Default gives the borrower twenty days to cure the default. If the borrower fails to cure the delinquency within the twenty day period, at least twenty one days before the scheduled sale date, the lender must record a Notice of Sale in the County Clerk's office, post the recorded Notice of Sale on the courthouse door, and mail a copy to the borrower at his last known address.

After all notice requirements have been met, the lender will con-

duct a public auction on the courthouse steps. The auctions are held on the first Tuesday of each month even if it is a legal holiday. The property will be sold to the highest bidder. If there are no bids, the lender may bid by canceling the debt and taking title to the property.

Under Texas law, there is no redemption period. Moreover, if the amount received by the lender at the auction is less than what was owed on the debt, the lender may seek a deficiency judgment against the borrower. The amount of the deficiency judgment is limited by law to the difference between the amount received at the auction (or the fair market value) and the outstanding balance on the loan (including late fees, attorney's fees, and the costs of conducting the auction).

If the lender chooses not to seek a deficiency judgment or agrees as a part of a loan modification or short sale not to seek a deficiency judgment, there are instances where the debtor must show the amount of the forgiven debt as income on his tax return. In instances where the lender has forgiven mortgage debt, it will send the homeowner a 1099 showing the amount of debt that was forgiven.

5.6.1 Who May Foreclose

In the most simple terms, the mortgagee (the lender) has the right to foreclose. Many mortgage loans get assigned multiple times. An assignment occurs when the current lender or loan servicer sells the loan to another company. When this type of transactions occurs, the seller lender should execute and record a document called an "Assignment of Mortgage" or similarly titled document. Unfortunately, many lenders fail to complete this step of the process which may jeopardize an assignee's right to foreclose if it is unable to demonstrate that it is the legal owner of the loan.

Another phenomenon which complicates the foreclosure process is the mortgage securitization process where loans are divided up into pieces and sold to various investors. This process makes it possible for one loan to have multiple owners.

Many borrowers have successfully challenged foreclosure actions on the basis that the purported lender did not have a legal right to foreclose because it either did not own the loan or could not prove its ownership of the loan. A successful challenge to a foreclosure, at worst, buys the borrower some time to make arrangements to find another place to live and, at best, gives the borrower leverage to force the lender to modify the loan terms.

5.6.2 What Happens After the Foreclosure Sale

Once the lender forecloses, the borrower has no choice but to vacate the premises. If the homeowner fails or refuses to vacate the property, the new owner will initiate eviction proceedings. State law governs the eviction process.

Many homeowners don't vacate the property because they don't have the financial wherewithal to move or because they have no where to go. In far too many instances, these homeowners are forcibly removed from the property and their belongings set out on the street. This has become a very sad reality in our country and is yet another reason that homeowners facing foreclosure must be proactive in finding a solution to their financial problems.

5.7 Is it Possible to Stall or Even Stop a Foreclosure?

If you have received a Notice of Default, the clock is ticking and you have a very limited amount of time to act to stall or stop the foreclosure. At this point, a distressed homeowner has very few options. The first option is to cure the default (bring the loan payments current). Some borrowers liquidate other assets, borrow money from friends or family, or borrow against retirement or insurance to bring their mortgage current.

Another option is to attempt to negotiate a loan modification or forebearance with the lender. It's important to know whether your lender will stop the foreclosure while it is considering your loan modification or forebearance request.

Some borrowers choose to sell the property. Because a short sale must be approved by the lender and that approval process can take a month or more, it's imperative to know whether the lender will stop the foreclosure while the sale is pending. Some lenders may only agree to stop the foreclosure if the homeowner agrees to pay the accrued attorney's fees and costs incurred by the lender in its preparations to foreclose.

Giving the property back to the lender is also an option. A homeowner may surrender the property to the lender by signing a deed in lieu of foreclosure. However, this can only be done with the lender's consent.

A final option is bankruptcy. When a bankruptcy petition is filed, the automatic stay immediately goes into effect. The automatic stay prevents creditors from making any collection efforts against a debtor, including foreclosure. Even if your case is utlimately dismissed without discharge, bankruptcy gives you a chance to get your affairs in order, find a new place to live, and move out.

Each of these options will be discussed in detail later on. So, please keep reading!

5.8 How Did We Get Here?

The media and the banking industry would have us believe that our economy, in general, and the real estate market, in particular, is in the precarious position it's in due in large part to irresponsible homeowners who bought more house than they could truly afford. But you know the truth now. The banks and greedy Wall Street brokerages played a part in creating this mess. They duped you into choosing a high risk loan option. They tricked you into believing that you'd be able to refinace into a fixed rate loan in a few years. They made you believe that your property value would skyrocket. Well, none of it was true and now you're paying the price – a huge price that's costing you sleep, putting a strain on your relationship, and placing your health in jeopardy.

That being said, any family in financial crisis should not wait around for the government to come up with a solution. Even when the government puts forth a viable means for homeowners to get the help they need (like the Making Home Affordable Program), lenders refuse to participate. So, it's obvious that turning to your lender may not get you the results you hope for and so desparately need. So, where does that leave you?

You need to form a partnership with someone who has your best interests at heart. You need someone who will be committed, over all else, to helping you solve your financial problems. That's where Lee Law Firm comes in. Our firm has helped thousands of families get the fresh start they deserve. We've helped these families save their homes from foreclosure and given them the piece of mind that everything will, indeed, be okay!

Foreclosure is terrifying! It means the loss of stablity and security. For most homeowners, it represents the loss of their biggest and most valuable asset. If I told you there's a way to stop the fore-closure, would you give us a call? If I told you that we will talk to your lender and aggressively work to find the best solution for you, would you give us a call? I hope so!

There are no guarantees in this life, but Lee Law Firm has a proven track record of helping families in financial crisis.[11] We have the experience and tools necessary to give our clients the best chance of getting a positive resolution to their problems. We are steadfast in our commitment to resolving even the most complicated financial matters. To that end, we work with all types of clients – from wealthy clients who have lost their fortunes to blue collar workers who've been laid off from their jobs. No case is too big or too small for the attorneys at Lee Law Firm!

9 Review

Regardless of how you got to this place, you need help. You need a viable solution that will end the stress and uncertainty that you are currently experiencing. You don't want to fight this battle alone. You need a partner who will be committed to protecting your best interests. You need a partner who can and will go toe to toe with your creditors and not back down. Lee Law Firm is the part-ner you need.

Lee Law Firm is committed to providing you with top-notch legal services. We will tailor an action plan specific to your case. We do this because we respect you and understand that your cir-cumstances and goals are unique to you. Before we can formulate your financial recovery plan, we will ask you a lot of questions about your finances. The following are a few of the questions we will ask you at your initial consultation:

- Has the Lender ever waived its right to require the payments be made on time by accepting and posting late payments in the past? (*Give Month and Day when the Lender allowed your late payment to be processed*)

- Is the Lender improperly attempting to pursue a Power of Sale Foreclosure? (*Please explain your reasoning*)

- Has the Lender ever been accused or found guilty of failing to comply with state foreclosure notice requirements? (*You may have to do some research to answer this question. However, Lee Law Firm is prepared to do that research for you, if necessary.*

- Has the Lender ever violated a state moratorium on fore-closures? (*Again, Lee Law Firm will handle this research if it is necessary to advance your case.)*

- Has the Lender ever violated the state or federal consumer protection laws, truth-in-lending laws, or the Real Estate Settlement Procedures Act (RESPA)? (*Lee Law Firm will handle this research if it is necessary to litigate your case.)*

- Is the loan usurious under state law?

- Has the Lender committed fraud or made misrepresentations in connection with the loan?

- Is the loan balance correct or has the lender failed to properly credit your mortgage payments?

- Is the Lender a part of a racketeering enterprise that has engaged in collection of unlawful debt?

- If the answer to any of these questions is "yes", you may have grounds to challenge the legality of the foreclosure.

Getting the answers to these questions is not always easy. That's why you need Lee Law Firm on your side. We want to be your partner and we are committed to fighting to save your home from foreclosure as zealously as if we were fighting to save our own homes!

CHAPTER SIX

Legal Challenges to Foreclosure:
The Uphill Battle to Save Your Home

Courts are hesitant to issue injunctions and restraining orders to stop foreclosures while borrowers make challenges to their legality. That's why bankruptcy can be so important in protecting your rights and saving your home. When you file bankruptcy, the automatic stay immediately goes into effect. The automatic stay prevents all of your creditors, including your lender, from pursuing collection efforts against you. This includes a foreclosure.

Once the automatic stay goes into effect, the lender must file a Motion for Relief from Automatic Stay and obtain an order from the bankruptcy court authorizing it to proceed with the foreclosure. Once that motion is filed, your attorney will file a response and raise any issues which represent valid challenges to the lender's right to foreclose.

6.1 Legal Challenges to Foreclosure

Ownership of the Loan

Many borrowers have been successful in challenging foreclosures on the ground that the foreclosing lender doesn't actually own the loan. Because of how loans are parcelized and sold to investors, it's often quite difficult to identify the owner (or owners, as the case may be) of the loan. Some courts have refused to allow loan servicers to foreclose because, under the law, loan servicers may not have standing (the legal right) to foreclose. Only the legal owner of the loan can foreclose. Ownership is proven by producing the promissory note or a properly executed and recorded loan assignment. If a foreclosing lender or investor cannot produce either of these documents, it may be forced to modify the borrowers loan.

Truth-in-Lending Violations

Federal truth-in-lending laws, known as the Truth-in-Lending Act (TILA), require mortgage lenders to disclose the actual cost of mortgage loans to borrowers.[12] Truth-in-lending disclosures must be made clearly and conspicuously, in a meaningful or understandable sequence, in writing, and in a form which the borrower may keep.

A lender who violates truth-in-lending laws is liable to the effected borrower regardless of whether the borrower was actually harmed by the violation unless the lender corrects the violation within 60 days of discovery of the violation and prior to any written notification, demand, or lawsuit from or by the borrower and the error occurred despite compliance with procedures reasonably adopted to avoid such violations.

Remedies available to borrowers whose lenders have violated truth in lending laws include:

- Rescission (cancellation of the contract)

- Actual and statutory damages
- Attorney's fees and court costs (where the borrower prevails in the lawsuit)

If a borrower rescinds a mortgage contract, he must pay back the money he borrowed. For most borrowers this simply is not feasible. However, a borrower who prevails in a lawsuit against a lender for truth-in-lending violations may be able to use the win as leverage to force the lender to modify the loan terms.

RESPA Violations

The Real Estate Settlement Procedures Act (RESPA) requires that certain disclosures be made to borrowers about the cost of settlement (closing) services and delineates guidelines for lender servicing and escrow account management. RESPA also requires the disclosure of business relationships between the various service providers involved in the settlement process.

A primary goal of RESPA is to eliminate unnecessary costs which make closing costs very high. Therefore, RESPA prohibits kickbacks and referral fees.

Common RESPA violations include:
- Failure to provide the borrower with a Good Faith Estimate;
- Failure to provide the borrower with a Mortgage Servicing Disclosure Statement;
- Failure to provide the borrower with an accurate HUD-1 Settlement Statement;
- Failure to provide the borrower with an Initial Escrow

Account Itemization;

- Failure to provide the borrower with an Annual Escrow Account Analysis Statement;

- Failure to provide the borrower with a Servicing Transfer Notice when the loan is sold.

Borrowers who believe their lender has violated a RESPA provision may file a civil suit or may file a RESPA complaint with the Office of RESPA and Interstate Land Sales, US Department of Housing and Urban Development, Room 9154, 451 7th Street, SW, Washington, DC 20410. Lenders that violate RESPA may also be subject to criminal penalties.

As with a truth-in-lending violations, you have the option of rescinding the loan when a lender has violated RESPA. Rescission would require you to pay the loan in full. If this is not feasible, you may be able to use a RESPA violation as leverage to force your lender to agree to a loan modification, short sale, or other workout plan.

Unconscionability

It's possible to challenge a foreclosure on the grounds that the terms of the loan or the circumstances surrounding the loan transaction are unconscionable. The word "unconscionable" essentially means unfair. But it's not enough to simply allege that the loan is unfair. For a foreclosure challenge based on unconscionability to succeed, you must be able to demonstrate that the loan was so unfair as to "shock the conscious" of the judge or jury.

Courts have found loans unconscionable where the borrower could not read, was not represented by an attorney, was pressured into the loan, and was unaware of important loan terms such as a prepayment penalty, adjustable interest rate, and balloon payment. A loan has also been found to be unconscionable where the borrower spoke little English and had no one present at the closing to translate and where the payments were so high that it was obvious he would default on the loan.

Servicing Errors

Loan servicers are notorious for making errors. Depending upon the severity of the error, you may be able to successfully challenge the foreclosure. Some of the most common errors loan servicers make include:

- Crediting payments to the wrong account;
- Charging excessive fees;
- Charging unauthorized fees;
- Miscalculating or overstating the amount necessary to reinstate the loan; and
- Mishandling escrow accounts.

If a servicer has made any of these errors, you may be able to use them against the lender to force it to agree to a loan modification. At the very least, a successful challenge based on servicing errors will force the servicer to recalculate what you owe. This recalculation could heavily impact your ability to reinstate the loan. If it turns out that you owe significantly less than what you were originally told, you may actually have enough cash available to reinstate the loan.

Breach of Contract

The promissory note and mortgage (deed or trust) you signed when you obtained your loan, set forth your duties and obligations with respect to the loan and the property. Moreover, those documents also set forth *the lender's* duties and obligations. If your lender has failed to act in accordance with the terms of the loan, you may have a claim for breach of contract.

Other Consumer Protection Violations

RESPA and TILA are two statutes meant to protect consumers, but there are numerous other consumer protection statutes upon which a challenge to foreclosure may be based. These include, but are not limited to:

- Home Ownership and Equity Protection Act (HOEPA);
- Fair Debt Collection Practices Act (FDCPA);
- Fair Credit Reporting Act (FCRA);
- Equal Credit Opportunity Act (ECOA).

Failure to Comply With State Foreclosure Procedures

Each state has specific laws which lenders must comply with when foreclosing on property. If a lender fails to follow the procedural requirements of the state in which the property is located, the borrower may have a legitimate basis for challenging the foreclosure.

Most judges will not stop a foreclosure (or set aside a foreclosure which has already occurred) if the lender's procedural errors were minor or if those errors did not actually cause harm to the borrower. On the other hand, judges are more likely to rule in the borrower's favor if the lender's violation of state foreclosure law is more serious, such as failing to follow statutory notice requirements.

These are only a handful of grounds upon which to base a challenge to foreclosure. Making these kinds of challenges to a foreclosure requires the knowledge and skill of an experienced attorney and the attorneys at Lee Law Firm have that knowledge and skill. We are among the most successful bankruptcy attorneys in Tarrant County and the surrounding area. We routinely assist clients in challenging foreclosures on the grounds discussed above and on numerous other grounds. We are familiar with all the dirty tricks lenders use to try to cheat people just like you out of their homes and we are fully equipped to litigate your case.[13]

6.2 Wrongful Foreclosures & Mortgage Servicer/Lender Abuses

Wrongful foreclosure is a tort generally available at common law. Historically, wrongful foreclosure cases have not been very successful. However, in recent years, due in large part to the rise in servicer and lender abuses and misconduct, more and more borrowers have been able to win these types of cases.

In a wrongful foreclosure action, the borrower typically alleges that the lender or servicer engaged in illegal, fraudulent, or willfully oppressive conduct in relation to making the loan, servicing of the loan or conducting the foreclosure sale. This conduct may relate to errors in the loan documents, incorrect interest rate changes, mishandling of escrow accounts, misapplication of payments, failure and refusal to communicate with the borrower about their loan, failure and refusal of the lender/servicer to adhere to the terms of a forbearance agreement, unnecessary forced place insurance, imposition of excessive or unauthorized fees, improper handling of accounts of borrowers with confirmed Chapter 13 plans, failure to follow state laws governing foreclosure sales, or errors or impropriety in how the foreclosure sale was conducted.

Borrowers who have been the victims of a wrongful foreclosure have several options:

- Seek a temporary restraining order (TRO) to stop the foreclosure sale before it happens;
- Seek a TRO to stop the eviction if the foreclosure sale has already occurred;
- Seek an order setting aside the foreclosure sale;
- File a wrongful foreclosure lawsuit seeking damages;
- File bankruptcy to stop the foreclosure and litigate the issues as part of the bankruptcy.[14]

Servicing issues may continue even after a borrower has paid his mortgage loan in full. One of the most common post-payoff abuses is the failure to provide the borrower with a satisfaction or release of mortgage evidencing that the loan has been paid in full. Many borrowers don't even know that they are legally entitled to receive such a document and do not become aware that having an open mortgage lien will impede their ability to sell or refinance the property or to obtain credit.

6.3 Lender/Servicer Errors and Abuses During Bankruptcy

It has also become increasingly common for mortgage servicing companies to make errors in crediting bankruptcy debtors' post-petition mortgage payments and to file motions for relief from the automatic stay in an effort to foreclose. This typically occurs as a result of the old industry standard of crediting payments received to the oldest outstanding balance. Adhering to this practice results in timely payments received post-petition being treated as if they are late. This practice is inappropriate when a debtor is in a Chapter 13 bankruptcy because the arrears are required to be paid through the Chapter 13 plan while post-petition payments must be paid directly to the lender.

Another common problem arises in relation to the handling of a Chapter 13 debtor's escrow account. In an effort to avoid violating the automatic stay, some lenders fail to notify debtors of escrow deficiencies. Under RESPA, borrowers are entitled to receive an annual escrow account reconciliation statement. Moreover, some states requires lenders to give borrowers written notice of escrow shortages within a specified period of time. Oftentimes, lenders fail to provide the borrower with the notifications required by RESPA and under state law, then seek to collect escrow shortages from the debtor prior to discharge or to have the automatic stay lifted so that they can foreclose. Courts have ruled in favor of debtors in these instances, stating that by failing to provide the annual escrow account statement and the required state notices regarding escrow deficiencies, the lender waived its right to collect the escrow shortages.

Issues may also arise in relation to how lenders calculate escrow shortages. In instances where the lender has paid escrow shortages over a number of years, they may base the next year's escrow requirements on the total accumulated deficiency. Additionally, if the lender has misapplied the debtor's post-petition mortgage payments, his escrow account could also be affected and appear to have a shortage.

Some lenders attempt to collect bankruptcy monitoring fees and other junk fees from Chapter 13 debtors. These fees may be labeled as inspection fees, property preservation fees, proof of claim preparation fees, and broker price opinion fees. If a lender attempts to collect any of these fees while the bankruptcy case is open, it does so in violation of the automatic stay.

Other common lender/servicer abuses include:
Failure to disclose bankruptcy monitoring and junk fees during the pendency of the Chapter 13 case;
Failure to follow applicable bankruptcy laws and rules for collec-

tion of these fees;

Collection of these fees post discharge when a debtor refinances or sells the property;

Including undisclosed attorney's fees in attachments to proofs of claim which include rules that say a failure to object by the debtor constitutes an acceptance of those fees;

Including unauthorized or excessive fees in the proof of claim.

There are literally dozens of dirty tricks that lenders and servicers use to cheat already strapped borrowers out of their money. As a layperson, you simply do not have the knowledge and experience needed to recognize or identify these bankruptcy monitoring and junk fees.

Think of your bankruptcy and your efforts to save your home from foreclosure as a war. You would never go to war without a strategy and an arsenal of weapons. The best and deadliest weapon you have in your fight against the mortgage company is a dedicated and determined attorney with the expertise to challenge the greedy, dishonest mortgage company at every turn.

6.4 What If The Foreclosure is "Lawful"?

There are times when there is no basis for a legal challenge to a foreclosure. Even when a foreclosure is lawful, there are foreclosure avoidance options available to homeowners. These options include:

- Selling the property;
- Loan Modification;

· · · ·

- Forbearance;
- Deed in Lieu of Foreclosure; and

  Bankruptcy.

6.5 Review

Challenging a foreclosure can be a very complicated and time-consuming process. You must understand who all the players in the process are and what they can do to assist you (or harm you) as you fight to save your home. You must also understand the various legal grounds upon which a foreclosure challenge may be based.

Because of the complex nature of a foreclosure challenge, it's imperative that you have an experienced attorney on your side. Don't try to fight the foreclosure alone. Most homeowners who do, eventually lose their homes. There's no guarantee that an attorney will be successful in saving your home from foreclosure. But, why risk it by trying to represent yourself against your lender?

You have so much at stake and you need the attorneys at Lee Law Firm on your side. We set the standard in successful client representation in the Tarrant County area and have a proven track record in assisting clients in resolving financial issues, including foreclosure challenges, through bankruptcy and other legal means.

12 Truth-in-Lending laws govern most consumer credit transactions.

13 If you don't live in the Tarrant County area, feel free to give us a call anyway. We can refer you to a bankruptcy law firm in your area that is as committed to helping their clients as we are.

14 A debtor may litigate a wrongful foreclosure action or any other issues which would ordinary be litigated in state court by filing an adversary proceeding. An adversary proceeding is a lawsuit filed within the bankruptcy and is heard by the bankruptcy judge

CHAPTER SEVEN

Where Do You Go From Here:
From Foreclosure Sale to Eviction

Your lender has foreclosed! Where do you go now? At this point, your situation has reached critical mass. If you don't move out of the home, you'll be evicted by the new owner of the property. In the most extreme instances, the sheriff or marshal will physically remove the homeowner and his family from the property and toss all their belongings in the street.

For many homeowners, moving after a foreclosure creates a whole new set of problems. Not only must they find a new place to live, they've got to come up with the money for a moving truck and for a security deposit and first month's rent. They may have to find a place to store some of their belonging and that costs money, too. They must make deposits for telephone service and utilities. For a family that has already hit rock bottom financially and which has no support network or other means of coming up with the money necessary to move, it's quite likely that they'll be evicted. Due to a lack of resources and the inability to formulate or carry out a plan, for some families, homelessness is the natural progression after a foreclosure.

7.1 Formulate a Plan

When you get behind on your mortgage payments, you must acknowledge that if you ignore the problem and do nothing, the end result is inevitable - *FORECLOSURE*! So, you must be proactive and the first step is to formulate a plan.

If your financial issues are temporary, you may be able to sell a few valuables or borrow money to bring your mortgage payments current. If your financial issues are more long term, you should contact a consumer attorney as soon as possible. He will explain your options to you and help you decide on a course of action. If bankruptcy is not the right option for you, you may decide to sell the property or you may negotiate a deed in lieu of foreclosure. You may be able to refinance or negotiate a loan modification. In some instances, you may be able to negotiate a loan assumption where a friend or family member assumes the loan and allows you to rent the property.

With any of these options, you need time, especially if you've already received the notice of default. That's why filing bankruptcy can be such a valuable tool. Filing bankruptcy may buy you the time you need to find a new place to live and get moved or to implement any of the other options which are available to you. Even if you ultimately decide that you simply cannot afford the house, bankruptcy affords you a means of surrendering it while at the same time stopping the collection efforts of *all* your creditors.

The next step in formulating your plan is knowing whether your state is a judicial foreclosure state or a non-judicial foreclosure state. If non-judicial foreclosures are authorized in your state, you need to ascertain when they are held. In Texas and Georgia, for example, non-judicial foreclosures are held the first Tuesday of each month. Once the foreclosure sale takes place, the clock quickly begins ticking and you have very little time to vacate the premises.

In judicial foreclosure states, it can take a year or more before the Court enters an order authorizing the foreclosure sale. If you live in a judicial foreclosure state you should use this time to save some money and payoff some other bills in the event the court authorizes the foreclosure and you must move.

Once the foreclosure takes place, the new owner will probably proceed quickly to evict you from the property. Depending upon the jurisdiction in which you live and how soon after the foreclosure the new owner begins the eviction process, you may have only a few weeks before the eviction takes place.

In some instances where the lender was the highest bidder at the foreclosure sale, you may be offered "cash for keys". Some lenders will offer a foreclosed homeowner cash money (usually between $1000 and $2500) in exchange for the keys to the property. A cash for keys agreement requires the homeowner to leave the property in "broom clean" condition. Cash for keys is a way for the lender to avoid the added costs of eviction while offering the homeowner an incentive to move. This cash incentive is especially attractive to homeowners who may not have the financial means to move.

Another benefit for lenders is that homeowners who enter into a cash for keys agreement seem much less likely to damage the property before vacating it, thus saving the lender money on repairs.

7.2 Carry Out Your Plan

Once you formulate a plan, you must actively work to carry it out. Time is of the essence. Whether you have partnered with an attorney, a foreclosure prevention company, a Realtor, or a debt counselor, it's imperative that you stay in regular communication with them. Additionally, you must stay in contact with your lender by providing regular updates about the progress you are making in carrying out your plan.

If you fail to communicate with your partner, it makes it that much more difficult for them to help you achieve your desired end result. If you fail to communicate with your lender, it leaves your lender little choice but to initiate foreclosure proceedings.

7.3 Redemption

Some states allow people whose homes have been foreclosed on a right of redemption.[15] During the redemption period, the homeowner has the right to redeem the property by paying the lender the outstanding balance on the loan, including principal, interest, late fees, attorney's fees and costs of foreclosure. If a third party purchased the property at the foreclosure sale, the homeowner exercises his right of redemption by paying that party the purchase price plus a percentage of the purchase price, as set by state law.

In most states which allow homeowners to redeem, the redemption period begins to run after the foreclosure sale. However, in a few states, the redemption period falls between issuance of the Notice of Default and the actual foreclosure sale. In either case, the redemption period can be as little as ten days or as long as five years.[16] During the redemption period, the homeowner may not be evicted from the property.

If you have questions about foreclosure or would like to explore your foreclosure avoidance options, visit our website at www.leebankruptcy.com to schedule a consultation.

7.4 Review

When a person is in a financial crisis, the natural inclination is to ignore the problem, believing that it will simply disappear or will magically resolve itself. Unfortunately, the world just doesn't work like that. That's why it's so important to be proactive in managing your financial crisis. Being proactive and taking action is empowering and will give you a sense of control.

You need to find the right partner to help you formulate a plan. And once you have a plan, you must actively work to carry it out. If you are facing foreclosure, time is of the essence. The sooner you begin working to resolve your financial issues, the more likely it is that you will be able to save your home from foreclosure or, at the least, find a resolution that best suits you. Even if you must sell your home or surrender it in bankruptcy or via a deed in lieu of foreclosure, having made the decision and done so on *your* terms will take a much lighter psychological toll than if your lender forecloses and you're evicted.

15   The following states have a redemption period: Alabama, Alaska (available on judicial foreclosures only), Arizona (available on judicial foreclosures only), Arkansas (available on
judicial foreclosures only), California (available on judicial foreclosures only), Connecticut
(decided by the Court on a case by case basis, Idaho, Illinois, Iowa, Kansas, Kentucky, Maine,
Maryland (decided by the Court on a case by case basis), Michigan, Minnesota, Missouri,
New Jersey, New Mexico, North Dakota, Oregon, South Dakota, Tennessee, Utah (decided by
the Court on a case by case basis), Vermont, Wisconsin, and Wyoming.

16   The redemption period in New Jersey is 10 days. In Minnesota, the redemption period is five
years.

CHAPTER EIGHT

Facing Foreclosure? You <u>DO</u> Have Options!

One of the biggest misconceptions struggling homeowners have is that they are at their lender's mercy. They think that the lender has the final say in what will happen to them and whether they will lose their home. The lender has a say, it just doesn't have the only say in whether the homeowner will be able to keep his home. You see, homeowners have options and by being assertive and proactive in exploring those options, you can position yourself so that you have as much control as possible over the disposition of your home when you are facing foreclosure.

8.1 Do Nothing

Doing nothing is an option only if you are current on your payments and you're underwater (you owe more on your mortgage than your house is worth). You can wait it out until the market turns around and your property regains some of the value its lost recently.

If you are behind on your mortgage, doing nothing simply is not a good option. If you ignore your lender's phone calls and letters, you're only delaying the inevitable. The lender will take your silence as an unwillingness to pay and will eventually begin the foreclosure process.

8.2 Forbearance

If your financial problems are temporary, you may be able to negotiate a forbearance agreement with your lender. A forbearance agreement will allow you to bring your mortgage payments current over a short period of time, usually six months to a year. For example, if your mortgage payment is $1500.00/mo. and you are two months behind, your lender may agree for you to repay the delinquency over six months. So, you would pay $2100.00/mo. for six months (your regular monthly mortgage payment of $1500.00 plus $500.00/mo toward the delinquency) until the loan payments are current. Depending on how large the mort-  gage arrearage is, the lender may require that you pay about 30% of the delinquency upfront and the balance over a short period of time.

A forbearance agreement may also involve the temporary suspension or reduction of mortgage payments. In these instances, any principal or interest that accrues during the forbearance period is added to the principal balance of the loan and will be due in a balloon payment at the end of the loan term.

In the typical forbearance agreement, the lender agrees not to foreclosure or make any other collection efforts against the borrower during the forebearance period as long as the borrower complies with all the terms of the agreement, including making all mortgage payments on time. If the borrower defaults under the forbearance agreement, the lender is free to initiate collection efforts against the borrower, including foreclosure.

Forbearance is not an appropriate option for anyone whose financial problems are long term. On the other hand, someone who has encountered a temporary financial setback, such as a accident or a short term illness, is an ideal candidate for forbearance.

Lee Law Firm offers a FREE forebearance agreement service for our clients. As a part of this service, we interview the client and draft the forebearance agreement. We forward the agreement to the lender or foreclosing attorney and will make two follow-up phone calls on behalf of the client. We will notify the client by phone of whether the forebearance agreement has been accepted, rejected, or ignored by the lender or foreclosing attorney.

8.3 Loan Modification

A loan modification is a negotiated remedy between a lender and a borrower which enables the borrower to remain in his home while eliminating the lender's need to foreclose because the borrower has defaulted on the loan. A loan modification typically involves permanently changing one or more of the loan terms in order it make the loan more affordable for the borrower.

In early 2009, the Obama Administration unveiled the Making Home Affordable Program meant to assist millions of homeowners who are struggling to make their mortgage payments. The Making Home Affordable Program also contains a refinance program to assist homeowners whose homes have lost value.

8.3.1 Who Qualifies for a Making Home Affordable Modification?

The Making Home Affordable Program is available to help struggling borrowers avoid foreclosure. The Making Home Affordable Program works in tandem with the Hope for Homeowners Program which was enacted in 2008 and modified in 2009 by passage of the Helping Families Save Their Homes Act.[17]

The eligibility requirements for the Making Home Affordable Program are as follows:

- The loan originated before January 1, 2009;

- The loan is a first mortgage on an owner-occupied property with a principal balance of $729,750 or less[18];

- Income must be fully documented with income tax returns and transcripts and the two most recent pay stubs;

- Borrowers must submit an affidavit of financial hardship;

- Incentives to borrowers who make their payments on time[19];

- Lenders and servicers receive an incentive for modifying loans where the borrower has not yet missed a mortgage payment.[20]

Owner occupany is verified through the borrower's credit report and other documentation such as utility bills. Investor-owned properties and those that are vacant or condemned do not qualify for the Making Homes Affordable program.

The Making Homes Affordable Program is available through

December 31, 2012. Under this program, loans can only be modified once.

According to the Huffington Post, as of September, 2009, only 12% of homeowners eligible to receive assistance under the Home Affordable Modification Program have received assistance. Lenders, such as Bank of America and Chase, claim that they have implemented their own modification programs to assist at-risk homeowners.

8.3.2 Home Affordable Refinance

Under the Making Home Affordable Refinance Program, assistance is available to homeowners with a good repayment history on existing mortgages owned by Freddie Mac or Fannie Mae. To qualify for a Home Affordable Refiance, the homeowner must be able to demonstrate that his home has lost value and now has less than 20% equity.[21]

Under the Home Affordable Refinance Program, eligible homeowners can refinance into a loan with a lower interest rate or, if they have an adjustable rate mortgage, can refinance into a 30-year fixed rate loan.

GSE lenders and servicers who offer assistance through the Home Affordable Refinance Program will not require as much documentation from borrowers because they already have much of the borrower's information on file.[22] Moreover, in some cases, an appraisal may not be necessary. These relaxed standards enable these refinances to be done much more quickly and at less expense to borrowers. The Home Affordable Refinance Program is available through June, 2010.

8.3.3 Preparing for Loan Modification

Lenders are overwhelmed by the number of loan modification requests. Many lenders will not even consider a loan modification request until they receive all requested documentation from the borrower. Therefore, it's important to be prepared before you ever make the first call to your lender. Following is some of the basic documentation you will need to provide to your lender:

- The most recent statement for the loan;
- The most recent statement for your home equity line or second and third mortgages, if applicable;
- The most recent statement for your homeowner's association, if applicable;
- Your most recent tax bill;
- Your most recent homeowner's insurance bill;
- At least one month's paystubs (profit and loss statement, if you are self-employed);
- Most recent W-2;
- Most recent tax return;
- Most recent monthly statements for credit cards, auto loans, student loans, and any other debts you may have;
- A detailed hardship letter explaining your financial situation;
- A budget showing your monthly income and expenses

including what you can reasonably afford to pay on your mortgage.

Whenever you have a conversation with a representative from your lender, be sure to document the call. Write down the date and time of the call, the name of the person you spoke with and what was discussed. You should also keep a copy of your hardship letter and supporting documentation which you submit to the lender with your loan modification request.[23]

8.4 Give the Property Back to the Lender

A deed in lieu of foreclosure is a means of surrendering the property to the lender without filing bankruptcy. Unlike a surrender of property in bankruptcy, your lender must agree to accept the deed in lieu of foreclosure.

A deed in lieu of foreclosure must be voluntary. In other words, a lender cannot force a borrower to sign a deed in lieu of foreclosure. For this reason, most lenders require a borrower who desires to negotiate a surrender of the property via a deed in lieu of foreclosure to make a formal written request which specifically states that the borrower wishes to voluntarily surrender the property.

In the past, lenders were unlikely to accept a deed in lieu of foreclosure where the value of the property was less than the amount owed on the outstanding mortgage. However, due to current market conditions, lenders will now often agree to accept a deed in lieu of foreclosure because it's likely they will end up foreclosing on the property anyway. By agreeing to accept a deed in lieu of foreclosure, lenders avoid the additional costs and delays associated with regaining possession of a property via foreclosure. Before a lender will agree to accept a deed in lieu of foreclosure, the borrower must demonstrate an inability to pay the mortgage. Most lenders will want to see the following documents from the borrower:

- The most recent statement for the loan;
- The most recent statement for your home equity line or second and third mortgages, if applicable;
- The most recent statement for your homeowner's association, if applicable;
- Your most recent tax bill;
- Your most recent homeowner's insurance bill;
- At least one month's paystubs (profit and loss statement, if you are self-employed);
- Most recent W-2;
- Most recent tax return;
- Most recent monthly statements for credit cards, auto loans, student loans, and any other debts you may have;
- A detailed hardship letter explaining your financial situation.

If you have a home equity line or a second or third mortgage, negotiating a deed in lieu of foreclosure will be much more difficult. You will have to get the subordinate lien holder to agree in writing to release its lien before your first mortgage holder will agree to accept the deed in lieu of foreclosure. In order to get the subordinate lien holder to agree to release its lien, you may have to agree to sign a promissory note whereby you'll continue to be obligated to repay that debt.

If you choose to negotiate a deed in lieu of foreclosure with your lender, it's imperative that you get a written statement from the lender that in exchange for your surrender of the property, it is waiving any rights it may have to collect a deficiency judgment against you. If you fail to obtain this assurance in writing, your lender may attempt to pursue a deficiency judgment against you.

8.5 Sell the Property

For homeowners who are underwater or who have very little equity in their property, a short sale may be the answer. A short sale, like a deed in lieu of foreclosure, is a negotiated remedy; both the lender and the borrower must agree to the terms. At the heart of a short sale is the lender's acceptance of less than what is owed as a full payoff of the mortgage.

Before a lender will agree to a short sale, the borrower must demonstrate his inability to pay the mortgage. To that end, the borrower must provide the lender with a number of documents which evidence his current financial situation. These documents include:

- The most recent statement for the loan;
- The most recent statement for your home equity line or second and third mortgages, if applicable;
- The most recent statement for your homeowner's

association, if applicable;

- Your most recent tax bill;
- Your most recent homeowner's insurance bill;
- At least one month's paystubs (profit and loss statement, if you are self-employed);
- Most recent W-2;
- Most recent tax return;
- Most recent monthly statements for credit cards, auto loans, student loans, and any other debts you may have;
- A detailed hardship letter explaining your financial situation.

You must list the property with a Realtor. So, the lender will want a copy of the Listing Areement and once your property is under contract, a copy of the Purchase and Sale Agreement. The lender will also want to review the Settlement Statement before closing. Once the lender approves the Settlement Statement any changes to it must be authorized by the lender.

In instances where there is a home equity line or other subordinate financing secured by the property, the first mortgage holder may offer the subordinate lien holder a cash incentive to release its lien. If the subordinate lien holder refuses to release its lien, the short sale will not go through.[24] In some cases, the subordinate lien holder will only agree to release its lien if the borrower signs a promissory note for the outstanding balance on the subordinate loan.

A short sale is a good option for anyone who is fairly certain that they won't be able to bear the cost of homeownership even if some or most of their other debts were eliminated. A short sale may also be a good option if your property has lost 40% or more of its value and you live in a neighborhood that was already in a state of decline before the real estate crash that began in 2007.[25]

8.6 Temporary Indulgence

Temporary indulgence is a grace period, usually 30 to 60 days, given by a lender to a borrower to bring the mortgage payments current or pay the loan in full. Temporary indulgence usually comes into play where the borrower is selling the property and the closing is imminent. It may also arise where the borrower is expecting a settlement, inheritance, or other lump sum distribution which he intends to use to bring the mortgage payments current.

8.7 Recasting

Recasting is a feature available in some mortgages which allows for the recalculation of the remaining principal and interest payments based on a new amortization schedule. Negative amortization loans typically contain a recasting provision. However, recasting may be available to distressed borrowers with other types of loans.

When a mortgage is recast, the interst rate may be reduced or the term of the loan may be extended. The goal is to make the loan more affordable to the borrower and to ensure that it will be paid in full at the end of the loan term.

8.8 Why These Options Often Don't Work

The primary reasons the above options don't work are lack of time and lack of communcation. Loan modifications, short sales, and other workout options take time. While the loss mitigation department is reviewing your workout request, the foreclosure department is moving forward as though the loss mitigation department does not exist. For whatever reasons, these two essential departments within your mortgage company often simply do not communicate with one another.

Time and time again, lenders foreclose on homes even though the loss mitigation department is reviewing a short sale application, a loan modification application, or a forebearance request. Many times, borrowers have paid money as a part of the process under the mistaken belief that the foreclosure would be cancelled while their workout request was being reviewed by the loss mitigation department. It's shameful, but it's true.

The other advantage bankruptcy has over these other options is that it gives debtor relief from the collection efforts of all his creditors. Bankruptcy gives a homeowner an opportunity to address credit card debt, medical bills, auto loans, tax debts, and other debts.

For these reasons, bankruptcy is the best option. Bankruptcy stops that foreclosure train in its tracks and gives a homeowner a chance to actually implement a plan to save their home from foreclosure.

8.9 Bankruptcy

The unique advantage of filing bankruptcy which the other options simply don't afford homeowners is the automatic stay. The automatic stay goes into effect the instant the bankrutpcy petition is filed and prevents *all* creditors from pursuing collection efforts against the debtor. This means that the mortgage holder cannot foreclose, the auto finance company cannot repossess the vehicle, and the credit card companies cannot sue you. Moreover, all collection letters and phone calls will also stop.

Bankruptcy affords a homeowner the benefit of being able to implement and carry out a plan to avoid foreclosure without the pressure created by the constant barrage of calls and letters from the mortgage company. More importantly, however, bankruptcy offers special tools to homeowners to deal with their mortgages. These tools often enable a borrower to save their home from foreclosure while simultaneously eliminating or reducing certain liens on the property. Bankruptcy will be discussed in depth in the next chapter.

8.10 Review

The circumstances which lead to a mortgage default are unique for every homeowner. Whether you are on the brink of foreclosure due to a job loss, divorce, or medical problem, you must recognize that you have options. However, you need the assistance of an experienced attorney who can explain these options to you and advise you as to which options are best for you based on your circumstances.

Lee Law Firm has represented thousands of families facing financial crisis. We have the skills and dedication necessary to help you resolve your issues. We are committed to providing superior and individualized representation to each and every one of our clients. All we ask of you is that you commit to being honest with us and with yourself about your circumstances and your goals and that you be responsive to our phone calls and e-mails. After all, we believe you deserve a fresh start and will do everything in our power to ensure you get it!

[17]   The Hope for Homeowners Act of 2008 allows qualifying homeowners to refinance into 30-year fixed rate FHA loans.

[18]   Higher limits are allowed on 2-4 unit, owner-occupied properties.

[19]   Borrowers who make their payments on time may receive a principal reduction of up to $1000.00 per year for five years.

[20]   Lenders and investors will receive a bonus incentive of $1500.00 and servicers will receive a bonus of $500.00 for each modification made while the borrower's payments are still current. Servicers may also receive an up front-fee of $1000.00 for each modification as well as "pay for success" fees of $1000.00 per year on still-performing loans.

[21]   Equity is the difference between a home's value and what is owed on all liens against the home.

[22]   GSE (Government Sponsored Enterprises) lenders focus on properties with government backed loans. Freddie Mac, Fannie Mae, FHA, and VA are examples of GSE lenders.

[23]   Never submit your originals to the lender because you will never get them back. I recommend keeping copies of the documents you submit so that you will have a complete and identical package of what you submitted to the lender.

[24]   The possibility of bankruptcy may be used as leverage to get a subordinate lien holder to agree to a short sale. If the borrower files a Chapter 7 bankruptcy and the property is worth less than what is owed on all loans secured by the property, the subordinate lien(s) will be treated as unsecured. If the debtor surrenders the property, the subordinate lien holder will get nothing. If the borrower files a Chapter 13, he may be able to avoid the subordinate lien if the house is worth less than the total of all liens on the property.

[25]   If it's unlikely that your property will regain its lost value within the next five to ten years, it might be best to do a short sale. You must do a cost benefit analysis and decide whether it makes good financial sense for you to continue to make mortgage payments on a home that is worth significantly less than what you paid for it and what you owe on it.

CHAPTER NINE

The Bankruptcy Option

Bankruptcy is meant to give financially overwhelmed consumers a fresh start. For homeowners facing foreclosure, bankruptcy can be one of the most powerful weapons in their arsenal. However, for many people, bankruptcy is taboo. They fear that their friends and family will think they are deadbeats. They fear that they will lose everything they've got. They fear their credit will be permanently destroyed.

Well, guess what? According to USCourts.gov, in 2008, 1,074,225 consumer bankruptcies were filed in this country and there were over 1 millions consumer bankruptcies filed during the first 9 months of 2009. So, you can see that there are lots of people taking advantage of the relief available under the bankruptcy laws of this country. These people are not deadbeats. They are hardworking people just like you who have run into unexpected financial problems. They are people just like you who want to pay their bills, but simply don't have the financial wherewithal to do so. *They are people just like you who need and deserve a fresh start.*

9.1 What is the Automatic Stay?

If you are facing foreclosure, bankruptcy is the most aggressive means you have of fighting it. When you file bankruptcy, the automatic stay goes into effect. The automatic stay prohibits your creditors, including your lender, from pursuing any collection efforts against you. This means they can't call you, send you letters, repossess your car, or foreclose on your home.

Imagine the relief you will feel once those harassing phone calls stop. Imagine the relief you will feel knowing that you have time to implement a plan to solve your financial problems. That's what the automatic stay gives you – time and space to put your plan into action.

9.2 Types of Bankruptcy

Consumer bankruptcy cases fall into two main categories: Chapter 7 and Chapter 13.[26] Whether you file a Chapter 7 case or a Chapter 13 case, the automatic stay becomes effective the moment your bankruptcy petition is filed with the court.

9.2.1 Chapter 13 Bankruptcy

Chapter 13 is a debt consolidation plan that allows a debtor to restructure his debt and pay it over a three to five year period. The debtor must propose a feasible Chapter 13 plan which sets forth how the debtor will pay both his secured and unsecured debts. A debtor must have sufficient income, after paying all his monthly expenses, to pay into the Chapter 13 plan.

The funds paid into the Chapter 13 plan will be used by the bankruptcy trustee to pay the administrative costs of the case, the debtor's attorney's fees, priority claims, such as taxes and child support, secured claims, such as mortgage arrearages and auto loans, and unsecured claims such as medical bills and credit cards. Once a debtor files bankruptcy, he must begin making his regular monthly mortgage payments as they come due beginning the first month after the petition is filed. The debtor must provide proof of all post-petition mortgage payments to the bankruptcy trustee in order for this Chapter 13 plan to be confirmed.

The debtor must begin making plan payments immediately and must make all plan payments which become due between the date of filing and the date of the confirmation hearing.[27] The debtor must provide the trustee with evidence of all Chapter 13 plan payments which become due between the date the petition was filed and the date of the confirmation hearing.

9.2.1.1 Creditor Claims and Debtor Objections to Claim in Chapter 13 Cases

To participate in and be paid through the Chapter 13 plan, creditors must file a Proof of Claim. The Proof of Claim must set forth the name and address of the creditor, the nature of the debt, the basis for the claim, the date the debt was incurred, whether the claim is secured or unsecured, and if it's secured, the type and value of the collateral securing it. Copies of documents evidencing the debt must be attached to the proof of claim. Proofs of claim must be filed within 90 days of the first date set for the meeting of creditors. However, governmental agencies are given 180 days from the first date set for the meeting of creditors during which to file a proof of claim.

Debtors have the right to object to all proofs of claim filed by creditors. This right is especially important for debtors who dispute how much they owe on a debt. In the case of mortgages, it is very common for lenders and servicers to make errors, sometimes substantial, in calculating loan balances. Moreover, it is not uncommon for lenders and servicers to charge unauthorized or illegal fees. For these reasons, it is imperative to review each proof of claim with a fine toothed comb.

If a debtor files an Objection to Claim, the lender must respond within a specified period of time and/or appear at the hearing. If the lender fails to respond to the debtor's objection or fails to appear at the hearing, its claim will be disallowed. This means that the creditor will be prohibited from participating in the plan.

9.2.1.2 Chapter 13 and Foreclosure Avoidance

As in Chapter 7 cases, when a debtor files a Chapter 13 bankruptcy the automatic stay goes into effect, preventing his lender and other creditors for pursuing any collection efforts against him. In order to move forward with a foreclosure, the lender must obtain an order relieving it from compliance with the automatic stay. Until such time as an order lifting or terminating the automatic stay is entered, the lender *cannot* foreclose. So, the immediate result of filing a Chapter 13 case is stop the foreclosure.

When a debtor files a Chapter 13 case, his lender cannot force him to pay all past due amounts in a lump sum in order to reinstate his mortgage. Chapter 13 bankruptcy affords the debtor the opportunity to cure the mortgage arrearage during the life of the Chapter 13 plan. For some borrowers the chance to pay the arrearage over time is all they need. For others, alternative provisions of the Bankruptcy Code must be utilized to ensure these they receive their fresh start they deserve. And that's where lien stripping comes in. There are two methods of lien-stripping: 1) Strip-down and strip-off. Strip-down refers to the process of reducing the value or amount of a secured lien down to the value of the collateral securing it. In strip-down cases, a lien is split into two portions: secured and unsecured. The unsecured portion of the lien can be avoided. For example, if the collateral is valued at $270,000 and the allowed claim is for $300,000, the loan will be split into a secured portion of $270,000 and an unsecured portion of $30,000. The $30,000 unsecured portion of the lien can be avoided.

Strip-off is the process whereby a lien is removed from a property because the value of the property is insufficient to secure the lien. For example, if the collateral is valued at $270,000 and the first allowed secured claim is for $270,000 and the second allowed secured claim is for $30,000, the second secured claim will be stripped off and treated as an unsecured claim.

Strip-off is particularly useful to debtors with underwater mortgages. Because a stripped off lien is treated as unsecured, depending upon the debtor's circumstances, it's quite possible that the holder of the stripped off junior lien will be paid little or nothing through the Chapter 13 plan. The end result for debtors with underwater second and third mortgages is a substantial reduction in their total debt load.

9.2.2 Chapter 7 Bankruptcy

Chapter 7 bankruptcy allows a debtor to liquidate most of his unsecured debt. However, not everyone qualifies to be a Chapter 7 debtor. To be a Chapter 7 debtor, a person must satisfy a certain threshold called the median income test. Under the median income test, a debtor must demonstrate that the total income for his household is less than the median income for a household of the same size in his state. If a prospective debtor satisfies the median income test, he may file a Chapter 7 bankruptcy.

If a prospective debtor cannot satisfy the median income test, there is a presumption that he has the ability to pay at least a portion of what he owes to his unsecured creditors. However, he may overcome that presumption by passing the means test. In a nutshell, the means test requires the debtor to demonstrate that his monthly expenses for housing, transportation, utilities, food, clothing, etc. are within the national and local standards as determined by the Internal Revenue services and once he pays those expenses, he would have nothing left to pay into a Chapter 13 plan. If a debtor cannot satisfy the means test, he will be required to pay at least $100.00 per month into a Chapter 13 plan for six years.

9.2.2.1 Chapter 7 and Foreclosure Avoidance

As previously discussed, the first benefit of filing bankruptcy is that the automatic stay which prevents creditors from pursuing collection efforts against a debtor goes into effect. The automatic stay has the immediate impact of stopping a foreclosure which is very valuable to a debtor facing foreclosure.

Unfortunately, the automatic stay does not stop a foreclosure indefinitely. If the lender files a Motion for Relief from Stay and that motion is granted, the lender may proceed with foreclosure proceedings.

A Chapter 7 debtor has several options when it comes to resolving a mortgage delinquency. One of the first questions which must be answered is whether the debt is a purchase money debt. If the debtor obtained the loan in order to purchase the property, it is a purchase money debt. If the loan was not obtained to purchase the property, in other words the loan is a refinance, it is not a purchase money debt.

If the debtor's mortgage is a purchase money loan, he has four options. The first option is to reaffirm the debt. When a debtor reaffirms a debt, he agrees to repay the debt pursuant to the original loan terms or new terms as negotiated with the lender. When a debtor reaffirms a debt, that debt is not discharged; if the debtor later defaults on the debt, the lender has the right to collect against the property and the debtor.

The next option for a Chapter 7 debtor with a purchase money mortgage is redemption. To redeem the property, the debtor must pay the creditor an amount equal to the value of the property. For most debtors, redemption of a home is not possible because they don't have enough cash available to make the lump sum payment to the creditor.

The third option for a Chapter 7 debtor with a purchase money mortgage is to surrender the property. Surrender is an especially useful option if a borrower is substantially upside down and has little prospect of regaining the lost value of this property within the next few years. If the debtor has subordinate financing that is wholly unsecured as a result of a decline in the value of the property, surrendering the property is a means of eliminating the subordinate financing while simultaneously circumventing the subordinate lien holders ability to collect on the debt.[28]

A final option for a Chapter 7 debtor with a purchase money mortgage is to make voluntary payments. If the debtor's mortgage payments are current, he can continue making those payments without reaffirming or redeeming the debt. If the borrower chooses to make voluntary payments, the debt will be discharged. If the debtor later defaults, the lender may take possession of the property via foreclosure, but is prohibited from making any collection efforts, such as a deficiency judgment, against the debtor.

In some jurisdictions, a Chapter 7 debtor may avoid a junior (or subordinate) mortgage lien on real property if the lien is partially or completely unsecured. In other jurisdictions, avoidance of junior liens securing real property is prohibited. The case law governing lien avoidance is very complex. Therefore, it's imperative that any debtor who wishes to avoid a lien retain experienced bankruptcy counsel to represent him.

9.3 Bankruptcy Exemptions

The Bankruptcy Code allows debtors to exempt or exclude from the bankruptcy estate certain property deemed necessary for everyday life and to facilitate a fresh start. Exemptions are provided under both state and federal law and which exemptions a debtor must use is determined under the law of the state in which the debtor lives. In Texas, debtors may use either the state exemptions or the federal exemptions.

9.4 Discharge vs. Dismissal – Why You Need Lee Law Firm

A debtor receives a discharge when he has successfully satisfied all requirements under the bankruptcy laws, and if he filed a Chapter 13, his Chapter 13 plan. Once a debtor receives a discharge, he is no longer personally liable for any debts which were discharged in the bankruptcy. This means that his creditors cannot pursue collection efforts against him for any of these debts. If, after receiving a discharge, he defaults on a secured debt which was not paid in full during the bankruptcy, the creditor has the right to repossess, foreclose, or otherwise regain possession of the collateral.

When a bankruptcy case is dismissed, the debtor returns to a pre-petition status with his creditors. It's as though he never filed bankruptcy. His creditors may immediately resume all collection efforts and legal remedies against him.

Bankruptcy cases in which debtors represent themselves, known as pro se cases, are dismissed more often than cases where debtors are represented by attorneys. The reason for this is that pro se debtors simply don't understand the complexities of bankruptcy law and their lack of knowledge leads to mistakes which they don't know how to fix. This inability to correct errors and to comply with the Bankruptcy Code leads to dismissal of their cases.

The best way to ensure you receive a discharge rather than have your case dismissed is to have an attorney representing you. There are lots of websites which offer do-it-yourself bankruptcy forms and there are numerous professional petition preparers, but these services are no substitute for an experienced bankruptcy attorney.

The stakes are extremely high; if your case is dismissed, you could lose your home, be subjected to lawsuits filed by your creditors, have your wages garnished and your personal property levied upon and sold to pay your debts. Don't leave your future and your security and stability to chance by representing yourself. Yes, an attorney costs money! But you're making an investment in your future. Wouldn't you rather pay an attorney who has your best interests at heart and who wants to help you save your home from foreclosure and help you solve your financial problems, than to deal with all the demands being made by your creditors? By now you must realize that VISA and Mastercard could not care less whether you and your children have a roof over your heads and food to eat. They are not in the least bit concerned about your health problems or that your spouse just died. All they want is their money. They truly expect you to pay them before you pay your mortgage.

The good new is that you can use bankruptcy to your advantage! You can push those greedy credit card companies to the very back of the line and focus all of your attention on saving your home from foreclosure. But you can't do it alone. You need an experienced and dedicated attorney on your side. Lee Law Firm is the preeminent bankruptcy law firm in Tarrant County. We have the legal expertise to represent you! We want to help you save your home from foreclosure and will formulate a plan that will achieve that goal and move you from financial crisis to financial stability.

9.5 Review

Bankruptcy is the strongest weapon a debtor has in fighting a foreclosure. Not only does bankruptcy afford you the protection of the automatic stay, it provides you with a venue for litigating any claims you may have against your lender via an adversary proceeding.

But filing bankruptcy should not be taken lightly. There are complex rules you must follow and strict deadlines to which you must adhere. You are in a fight to save your most valuable asset and to obtain the fresh start that you truly deserve. Therefore, you must be prepared to assist your attorney every step of the way by providing honest answers to his questions and by providing him with all the documents and information he requests from you in a timely manner. You must be prepared to appear at every meeting and hearing. Missing a court date could make the difference between getting the best possible result and having your case dismissed (which could be disastrous)!

---

26   Individual consumers may also file Chapter 11 bankruptcy, but rarely do so.

27   The debtor must attend a 341 meeting of creditors about 30-45 days after his bankruptcy petition is filed. The confirmation hearing usually takes place about 30-45 days after the meeting of creditors. At the confirmation hearing, the trustee will either recommend or object to confirmation of the debtor's Chapter 13 plan. If the trustee recommends confirmation, the court will accept that recommendation and enter an order approving the plan. If the trustee objects to confirmation of the plan, a hearing will be held and based upon the testimony and evidence presented, will enter an order approving or rejecting the plan.

28   If the subordinate loan is wholly unsecured because of a reduction in the value of the property, that loan will be treated as an unsecured debt and will be discharged along with the debtors other unsecured debts.

CHAPTER TEN

If You Wait Around for the Government to Help You, It May Be Too Late

Legislators continue to promise to revive legislation that would allow homeowners who file bankruptcy to modify their mortgages as part of the bankruptcy proceedings. President Obama's voluntary foreclosure prevention program has failed to deliver and many legislators are ready to get more aggressive with mortgage lenders.

Last year it seemed almost inevitable that legislation would pass allowing homeowners to modify their toxic mortgages during bankruptcy; but the measure fell 15 votes short of passage in the Senate. The bankruptcy bill had public strong support amongst voters; but the banking lobby strongly opposed the measure claiming that it would lead to substantially higher interest rates. However, because the banking industry has failed to stem the rise in foreclosures, have failed to offer homeowners assistance pursuant to the Hope for Homeowners and Making Home Affordable Programs, and have failed to deliver stimulus dollars to Main Street via mortgages and other loans, Senator Richard Durbin and other legislators are looking to put the measure back on the table for another vote.

Your situation is urgent! Therefore, you can't wait around for the government to offer up a solution. If you do, it will be too late. Remember, non-judicial foreclosures happen quickly and even if you're in a state that only allows judicial foreclosures, a government solution may not come before the court authorizes your lender to foreclose on your home. You must be proactive. You must find a partner, like Lee Law Firm, that appreciates the urgency and uniqueness of your situation. You need a partner who is committed to helping you find a solution now!

CHAPTER ELEVEN

Lee Law Firm's Commitment to You
Lee Law Firm is Committed to Helping Families in Financial Crisis

My name is Christopher M. Lee. I am the owner of Lee Law Firm, PLLC. I have been practicing law since 2003. My firm focuses in consumer bankruptcy and assisting families in financial crisis, including those facing foreclosure.

Many attorneys are general practitioners. This means they handle a variety of legal matters. These general practitioners may represent a few clients each year in bankruptcies, divorces and other family law matters, DUI's, personal injury cases, and criminal cases. Have you heard the saying "Jack of all trades, master of none"? Well, that's what a lot of general practitioners are. Because they practice so many different types of law, they never become experts in any one area.

That's not the case with Lee Law Firm. We handle thousands of bankruptcies each year and successfully assist numerous clients in overcoming financial crises. We are committed not only to showing our clients that there is a light at the end of the tunnel, but in helping them arrive at that light.

We take what we do seriously. When I started my law practice, I decided that the best way to help families was to focus in consumer bankruptcy law because so many people find themselves on the brink of financial disaster through no fault of their own. Whether because of the death of a spouse, a divorce, a major illness, or job loss, good people find themselves in bad situations and often don't know where to turn. Well, families living in Fort Worth and the surrounding areas are no longer alone. They have Lee Law Firm to assist them in finding the right solution to their financial problems.

The Goal of this Publication

The lives of too many hardworking Americans are thrown into chaos each year by unexpected events that have a devastating impact on their family finances. Experience has shown us that it's fairly common for people in financial crisis to go into denial. They think that if they ignore the problem, it will go away; it will magically solve itself. Unfortunately, that simply isn't the way life works and that's why I decided to write this book. My goal is to help struggling families face reality and begin implementing a plan to help them resolve their financial issues.

The first step is to acknowledge that there *are* solutions if you are struggling financially. You don't have to live in your current state of worry and fear indefinitely. If you make a commitment today to change your life and improve your situation, I guarantee that you will begin to feel better. By making the choice to take control and by partnering with Lee Law Firm, or a firm in your area with a similar commitment to its clients, you will regain your power and your dignity. Can you imagine how liberating that will be? And, that is the primary goal of this book – to empower you with the information you need to break free from the financial worries that are holding you back and set you on a course to financial freedom and living the life of your dreams!

We Can Help You Find Solid Ground

Do you want to secure a new future for yourself within the next two years? Do you want want to be able to wake up each morning with the knowledge that you are financially stable? If you answered "yes" to these questions, there's good news. You don't have to teeter on the edge of a financial precipice, wondering how you're going to pay your mortgage, buy groceries, or put gasoline in your car. Starting today, you can change your life and create your future – a future free from anxiety and worry over money and overwhelming debt.

Too many Americans are being forced to choose between buying their prescription medications and making their car payment. They are being forced to choose between buying groceries and heating their home. They are being forced to choose between paying for basic upkeep on their car and sending their child on class field trip. In addition to all this, collection agencies are ringing their phones of the hook with no regard for the difficult financial choices they face each and every day. The purpose of this book is to supply you with the information you need to get out from under the debts that are suffocating you and to help you get the fresh start you deserve. I'm going to show you how to find solid ground and get your feet back under you!

Think of me as your partner. As your partner, my responsibility is to educate you and advocate for you. I am offering you a solution to your financial problems and I'm here to help you and your family. My firm is committed to helping you secure solve your financial problems and return to a life of financial stability.

How Can Lee Law Firm Help Your Family?

Over the past 10 years, Lee Law Firm has represented thousands of clients in financial crisis. By virtue of our extensive experience, we have learned how to ask the right questions so that our clients speak openly and honestly about their financial situation. As a result, we are able to help our clients understand the extent of their financial situation and how important immediately formulating a plan truly is to making a fresh start.

Take a few moments to answer the following questions. Doing so, is the first step to evaluating your financial health.

1. What is your current monthly household income?
   $_____

2. What is the principal balance on your mortgage?
   $_____

3. How much is your monthly mortgage payment?

$_____

4. What is the appraised value of your home?
   $_____

5. On average, how much do you spend on groceries and other household items each month? $_____

6. On average how much do your utilities cost you each month? $_____

7. How much do you owe on your credit cards? $_____

8. How much do you pay on your credit cards each month? $_____

9. How much do you still owe on your auto loan? $_____

10. How much do you owe on your student loans? $_____

Most people who are struggling financially have no idea exactly how much they owe. However, by the time most individuals get to question seven or eight, they have a much better idea of how deep in debt they actually are. Seeing the numbers in black and white can be unsettling and extremely painful. But knowing the truth about what you owe is the first step to making the change you so drastically want. So, after looking at these questions and your answers, ask yourself, "Am I in a position to solve my financial problems and get out of debt without the assistance of a professional?" If you answered "no" to this question, then give us a call

- the attorneys and staff at Lee Law Firm are committed to helping you!

By Honestly Assessing Your Debt, You Assist Us in Helping You Find A Solution!

Whether you are seeking legal expertise because you are experiencing mild to moderate financial difficulties or are on the brink of financial disaster, it is important to honestly assess your situation. This means gathering all your bills, adding up how much you owe and your minimum monthly payments and comparing those numbers to your monthly income. You must also factor in your discretionary spending and cash expenditures to get a true picture of how much money you spend each month. Once you've made a realistic assessment of your monthly spending as it compares to your monthly income, the next step is to put a plan in place to help you get out of debt. That's where Lee Law Firm comes in. Whether you choose bankruptcy, debt consolidation, or some other solution, we will be with you every step of the way.

Lee Law Firm is dedicated to providing you with exceptional service. We believe that each of our clients is entitled to outstanding representation. To that end, at your initial consultation, you will meet with an attorney, not a paralegal or legal assistant. And from start to finish your case will be handled by an attorney. You will also work closely with our support staff as your petition is drafted. But understand that one of our experienced attorney's is at the helm and will remain abreast of every development in your case.

Because of our commitment to excellence and our outstanding customer service, the vast majority of our clients are referred to us by existing clients. Therefore, we take a special interest in making sure our clients get the best possible outcome under the circumstances. We work closely with each client to tailor a strategy customized to their particular circumstances. We never take a cookie cutter approach because we recognize that each client's situation and goals are unique.

Helping Good People Through Bad Times

That's our firm philosophy – *Helping Good People Through Bad Times*! We recognize that bankruptcy sparks intense emotions in many people. The credit card industry has spent billions of dollars to stigmatize bankruptcy. We at Lee Law Firm know that bankruptcy is a valid and necessary option for many people. We were the **largest volume filers** in Dallas and Tarrant County in 2008 and **2009 and dedicate ourselves to solely filing bankruptcy cases** which **includes stopping foreclosure** and **repossession** of your home and assets.

It is our experience that the best way to serve our clients is to devote all our time to one area of law. We chose bankruptcy as a specialty because anyone can find themselves in the midst of a financial crisis and bankruptcy law is a way to help people in a way that dramatically impacts their lives. It is a very rewarding experience to meet with a client in crisis who is facing the loss of their property, experiencing loss of sleep and loss of good will with friends and family members, and having the opportunity to improve their situation. Our number one goal is to assure that clients who visit with us benefit from our services and walk out of our office a new person with a fresh start. It is our experience that the average person is a job loss or an unexpected emergency away from the need for a bankruptcy attorney. All of our clients are good people that have been the victim of bad circumstances and we are 100% committed to helping them get to a better place – financially and emotionally.

Partner Bio

Christopher Lee was admitted to the State Bar of Texas in 2003, he received his law degree from Texas Wesleyan University in 2003, and graduated from Indiana State University in 1999 with degrees in political science and history. He is also a member of the American Bar Association, the Tarrant County Bar Association, the Dallas County Bar Association, the National Association of Consumer Bankruptcy Attorneys, the America National Bankruptcy Institute, the Dallas Association of Young Lawyers, the Tarrant County Young Lawyer Association, and the American Consumer Bankruptcy College.

Unlike a lot of attorneys that dibble and dabble in bankruptcy law handling a few bankruptcy cases a year, I decided when I started my practice to focus on bankruptcy law because I knew I could make the biggest difference in the lives of people in my community. I was concerned about the cyclical nature of the economy in Tarrant County and the surrounding areas and the devastating impact unexpected events such as a job loss can have on a family's finances. I also recognized that many people in the midst of crisis go into denial. By choosing to practice bankruptcy law, I knew I could offer proactive solutions and show clients that there is light at the end of the tunnel.

Lee Law Firm suggests that people who are falling behind on their mortgage payments seek consultation as soon as possible in order to avert a financial disaster. The attorneys at Lee Law Firm are so successful because they make it a habit to discuss mortgages and other financial issues with their clients in clear, easy to understand terms. We offer options to our clients and help them choose the one that is best for them.

How We Help You Get A Fresh Start

We are committed to working with you to develop and implement a plan to resolve your financial problems and get you the fresh start that you deserve. We want you to have a secure and stable future. But we can't achieve these goals without your assistance and your commitment to the process. We have to work as a team to formulate and implement a plan that will be the solid foundation of your financial future.

This partnership is grounded in constant communication. This means there will be plenty of phone conversations and e-mails throughout the process. We review the documentation you gather and supply to us and we will draft your bankruptcy petition and schedules and have you review them to ensure they are correct. After we file your petition and schedules, we will monitor your case and keep you informed as your case develops. We will file all necessary motions and respond timely and aggressively to all motions and other pleadings filed by your creditors.

Are you sick and tired of all the harassing and abusive calls from your creditors and bill collectors? Do you dread going to your mailbox each day because you know it will be filled with letters from collection agencies? Are you drowning in a sea of debt? If you answered "yes" to any of these questions, give us a call to today to discover how we can help you get a fresh start. A new and secure financial future is just a phone call away!

We Get to Know Our Clients and Their Goals

Rest assured, you are not alone. We are in this fight for your financial future each and every step of the way. Remember, we specialize in representing clients in financial crisis. This is what we do and we do it well! We are so successful because we take a personal interest in each of our clients. We get to know them and we help them set realistic goals and formulate a plan to achieve those goals. We help our clients regain control of their finances and get back to the business of living!

We Provide You With Resources That Other Firms Don't Offer!

We understand that the average person is a job loss, divorce, or illness away from financial disaster. When people are struggling financially, an unexpected expense such as a car repair or a broken arm can push them over the edge For this reason, we give our clients access to a variety of different resources.

As a result of having represented thousands of clients in financial crisis and hearing their stories, we began keeping a list of available social service agencies in the Tarrant County community and surrounding areas. From food banks to women's shelters, to Section 8 housing and other government assistance programs, we can immediately put our clients in contact with the agencies that can assist them. Our number one goal is to make sure our clients benefit from our services and all the available resources our community has to offer. This is the best way of ensuring that our clients get the fresh start they deserve.

How to Contact Us

Lee Law Firm,
8701 Bedford Euless Road, Suite #510
Hurst, Texas 76053
Website: www.leebankruptcy.com
E-mail: customerservice@leebankruptcy.com
Phone: 817-265-0123

CHAPTER TWELVE

Client Testimonials

A very great experience not knowing what to expect. It wasn't as bad as we thought it would be. We feel relief now knowing that we have a true expert staff to help us through our situation.

R. Crear

My appointment today was very good and informative. I really do appreciate the time and effort put into helping me get back into a new financial path.

F. Hernandez

They ensured me that my visit was not as scary as I had anticipated. I was VERY nervous as I drove in relentless traffic to arrive at my appointment 15 minutes late. They were not in the least put off by my tardiness. On the contrary, they were most helpful at putting me at ease and answering my incessant questions about bankruptcy (this being my first experieence with it). They patiently walked me through each question and document, providing answers and helping me fill in areas where the answer was not exactly what the question asked for (putting unemployment compensation in the right place is just one example). The meeting was handled professionally and with the utmost consideration of my current situation. If you have a Hall of Fame wall, put their pictures on it. If not, get one so these ladies can be recognized.

L. Lehrman

Dear Lee:

When I first got your foreclosure letter my wife and I were very upset and didn't know where to turn. In addition to your foreclosure letter we got a million other letters in the mail as well. Your letter stood out to me and I wanted to take you up on the offer to do a FREE forbearance. I was skeptical because I hear so much about forclosure scams and people being taken advantage of when they are facing this crisis. However, I took a chance and called your office. I spoke with Sherri to schedule the appointment just like it mentioned in the letter. She was so friendly and helpful and set me up an appointment.

I came into the office and everyone answered my questions and prepared the free forbearance offer as promised. I paid nothing for the service and to my great surprise the offer was accepted within two days of my initial appointment. I decided to decline the to go forward with the forbearance because in my circumstance a Chapter 13

bankruptcy turned out to be a better option
based on my financial situation. I felt good
about retaining Lee because they earned my
trust and did what they said they would do.
Thank you so much and I will recommend
you to anyone else having the same problem
I had.

Sincerely,

D. Hornes

There are many more testimonials online at

www.leebankruptcy.com

· · · ·